Dykes J. Oswald

The Laws of the Kingdom

Dykes J. Oswald

The Laws of the Kingdom

ISBN/EAN: 9783337166939

Printed in Europe, USA, Canada, Australia, Japan

Cover: Foto ©ninafisch / pixelio.de

More available books at **www.hansebooks.com**

THE
LAWS OF THE KINGDOM.

BY

J. OSWALD DYKES, M.A.

Μὴ ὢν ἄνομος Θιοῦ ἀλλ' ἔννομος Χριστοῦ.—1 COR. IX. 21.

NEW YORK:
ROBERT CARTER AND BROTHERS.
1873.

MURRAY AND GIBB, EDINBURGH,
PRINTERS TO HER MAJESTY'S STATIONERY OFFICE.

NOTE.

These pages are designed to form a continuation to a small work recently published on 'THE BEATITUDES OF THE KINGDOM.' *It is proposed to devote a third volume to the treatment, in similar style, of the rest of the Sermon on the Mount.*

CONTENTS.

PART I.

RELATION OF THE NEW LAW TO THE OLD.

	PAGE
GENERAL PRINCIPLE: FULFILMENT, NOT DESTRUCTION,	1
FIRST ILLUSTRATION: SIXTH COMMANDMENT,	21
SECOND ILLUSTRATION: SEVENTH COMMANDMENT,	43
THIRD ILLUSTRATION: OATHS,	63
FOURTH ILLUSTRATION: LEX TALIONIS,	85
FIFTH ILLUSTRATION: WHO IS MY NEIGHBOUR?	109

PART II.

THE LAW OF SECRECY IN RELIGION.

THE PRINCIPLE: BEFORE GOD, NOT MEN,	133
FIRST APPLICATION: TO ALMSGIVING,	151
SECOND APPLICATION: TO PRAYER,	173
EXCURSUS: THE MODEL PRAYER,	193
THIRD APPLICATION: TO FASTING,	217

PART I.

RELATION OF THE NEW LAW
TO THE OLD.

THE GENERAL PRINCIPLE:
FULFILMENT, NOT DESTRUCTION.

Think not that I am come to destroy the law or the prophets: I am not come to destroy, but to fulfil. For verily I say unto you, Till heaven and earth pass, one jot or one tittle shall in no wise pass from the law till all be fulfilled. Whosoever, therefore, shall break one of these least commandments, and shall teach men so, he shall be called the least in the kingdom of heaven; but whosoever shall do and teach them, the same shall be called great in the kingdom of heaven. For I say unto you, That except your righteousness shall exceed the righteousness of the scribes and Pharisees, ye shall in no case enter into the kingdom of heaven.—MATT. V. 17–20.

Cf. LUKE XVI. 17 : *It is easier for heaven and earth to pass than one tittle of the law to fail.*

THE GENERAL PRINCIPLE:

FULFILMENT, NOT DESTRUCTION.

IN the eight Beatitudes of the Kingdom with which the Sermon on the Mount opens, the spiritual King has defined who they are whom He numbers among His subjects. Of all who bear this blessed character He says, 'Of such is the kingdom of heaven.' But the bulk of this inaugural address of our Lord is legislation. Its main design was to lay down the constitutional principles or legal axioms of His spiritual kingdom. To this design a description of its blessed subjects could be only preliminary. Accordingly, the beatitudes are followed up by a series of legislative paragraphs, which, under several heads, cover the main duties of the citizen in God's new or Christian kingdom.

PART I.

GENERAL PRINCIPLE.

Matt. v. 3, 10.

Of these legislative sections, the first and most important is that which fills the remainder of St. Matthew's fifth chapter. It takes its form from the necessity under which this new Legislator found Himself to define His relation to the pre-

Matt. v. 17-48.

PART I.
———
GENERAL
PRINCIPLE.

ceding legislation of His nation. Jesus did not begin, no legislator ever does begin, to write His law, as it were, on clean paper. It is impossible for any religious reformer or founder to sweep the ground quite clear of all previous systems, or to begin to build up a system of his own without respect to his predecessors' work. Jesus found the Jewish people what the whole previous history of their fathers had made them; with a definite and venerable code of laws, and a very minute and pompous liturgy of sacrifice and praise. It was impossible not to begin by defining how His new kingdom stood related to the ancient theocracy of Moses and the prophets. He spoke as a Hebrew prophet to a Hebrew audience; and the very first question which met Him, or at least which lay unexpressed in the thoughts of every hearer, was this: You say you are come a teacher sent by God to set up among us a new kingdom. Other teachers we have had from God, who in our fathers' days, from Moses to Malachi, did set up our kingdom and gave us laws in abundance. What must we understand you to make of all this former revelation and these existing laws?

To this question there was the more need to give an immediate and explicit answer, because already His audience was divided by a false conception on the point. It was rumoured, and several things gave colour to the rumour, that the new Prophet's teaching was essentially destructive—hostile to, and meant to subvert, the good old system of law and rite delivered to the fathers through the hand of Moses. Two parties in the nation caught at this notion; the one in hope, the other in fear. While the mass of the common people, busy with field labour or with trade, were not ill-pleased to hear that the strict discipline and intolerably minute rubrics of the old law were to be relaxed; a smaller section, whose professional importance and reputation for sanctity rested mainly on their exceptional observance of legal punctilio, resented the infraction of the written code, even in a 'jot or tittle,' as sacrilege or apostasy. It was against this two-faced misconception Jesus had to guard His own position; and it was this which determined the two-faced form of His main statement:

> 'Think not that I am come to destroy the law or the prophets;
>
> 'I am not come to destroy, but to fulfil.'

Ver. 17.

These very weighty words, which condense for us this whole section of the discourse, are a protest, on the one side, against the blind spirit of revolt, the radical reaction, whose impulse is to tear itself loose from all that went before, and to destroy the good along with the evil in that which is; on the other side, against the rigid unprogressive conservatism, which in its idolatry of the past would arrest development, and which refuses to 'fulfil' the spirit of existing systems by a wise superseding of their form. Though these words were framed to meet the immediate prejudices of a Jewish audience, they enclose the golden rule of all progress. To the philosophic statesman and to the religious reformer of every generation, the best recommendation of what is new will always be that it comes not to destroy the old, but to fulfil it; to understand its spirit, to realize its purpose, to carry forward its work, and to make every change an unfolding into higher power of whatever truth or goodness had been the living soul of systems which, through lapse of time, are now grown old and 'ready to vanish away.'

It was through no accident that Jesus Christ held towards the Hebrew Old Testament this relation of a fulfiller, any more than it was by an accident that He Himself was born a Jew. Judaism was the divine preparative for Christianity. From the call of Abram to the coming of Christ is one unbroken historical process, and the special function of the elect people was to give birth to the new kingdom. It was out of the womb of Judaism, and only out of it, that, as its lawful offspring, Christianity could come. I take for granted, that when our Lord spoke of 'the law and the prophets,' He used a current phrase for the entire sacred literature which held the Hebrew economy of revelation. The writings, of course, are only of value as embodying a religion or system of truth and duty; and the division into 'law' and 'prophets' corresponds to the two sides of the Hebrew religion which were most characteristic of it: I mean its aspect of command or literal injunction, most felt by the least spiritual; and its aspect of promise or underlying hope, best seen by the most spiritual. Of these, the former certainly found its chief utterance in the Mosaic Pentateuch, the latter in the later prophetic books. But of the entire system from first to last, this was the great peculiarity, that while, in the words of a New Testament writer, 'the law made nothing perfect, there was still the bringing in of a better hope.'[1]

PART I.

GENERAL PRINCIPLE.

John iv. 22.

Heb. vii. 19.

---

[1] This is in substance Bleek's rendering (*Hebräerbrief*, ii. 350), slightly but not materially different from the marginal reading in our Authorized Version.

PART I.
GENERAL
PRINCIPLE.

Imperfection was its first mark, and that attached itself mainly to 'the law:' it perfected nothing. Preparation was its second, and belonged more to 'the prophets:' there was the bringing in of a better hope. Manifestly, these two are so connected, that it could not help being imperfect, just because it was preparatory. From this point it becomes easy to answer the vexed question about the completeness or perfection of the Old Testament system. Looked at in the light of its end, in view of that for the sake of which it existed, and towards which it led the world, it will seem, on any candid and liberal construction, to be a worthy product of His wisdom Who designed it; fit for its work, and completely answering the design of His gracious providence. But if any one will choose to examine its parts out of all relation to that which followed it, and to judge of them by a perfectly independent standard, it will not be hard to prove it in many ways faulty, defective, and amiss. It cannot help being so. That which is only meant to introduce something else

Cf. Heb. xi. 40.

and better, without which it cannot be made perfect, must of course look imperfect, and be imperfect, so long as it stands alone. It may be as good as it can be for the time and for its purpose; but it must be less good and less entire than the 'better thing' for which it waits. It is idle, therefore, to claim for the Old Testament such perfection as we claim for the New; or labour to explain away the inferiority of Judaism to Christianity. The Old stood in need, says Jesus, of fulfilment. Look at the Law apart from the Gospel: what is it? An imperfect code; a handful of moral enactments, which cover only a fragment of human life, coupled with arbitrary regulations about food and dress, and the colour and size of buildings, and the ritual of religious ceremony, which could only be kept in one very small corner of Syria, and which even there look absolutely puerile in themselves. The Levitical code, unfulfilled, is a fragment, shapeless, and without consistent meaning. Fulfilled in Christianity, it falls into its place; it dovetails in with its complement; it recovers its *rationale;* it grows intelligible. The whole Law, therefore, was in a sense prophetic; it foretold its fulfilment, for it craved it. The Ten Words craved a more spiritual interpretation, and the obedience which appeared impossible. The liturgy craved to be read in the light of a spiritual worship of atonement, offered for men by a more effectual Priest, in the real purity, not of white linen, but of a clean heart.

PART I.
———
GENERAL
PRINCIPLE.

The civil institutes of the little Shemitic commonwealth meant little for the earth, if there never was to be any wide spiritual kingdom of divine rule over all nations and the souls of all men. In short, the whole Hebrew system stood erect, with a finger pointing forward, as the guide and tutor of earlier ages to lead men's eyes onward to the world's better hope. Fulfilment was that mighty something for which it waited, to be the answer of its riddles, the supply of its wants, the substance of its symbols, the fact filling out its forms. That something was Jesus. When you know how much it means, and how long mankind had been kept waiting for it, there is sublimity in the composure with which this simple preacher of Galilee sets Himself forth as the Fulfiller: 'I am not come to destroy, but to fulfil.'

On the other hand, it must not be forgotten that all fulfilment of an imperfect by a more perfect stage of development involves what is a kind of destruction. In so far as the Old Testament was preparative of the New, it was temporary or destructible. It provided a perishable envelope for truth, which was as yet in the germ only; it threw athwart the world's path shadows from 'good things to come;' it created a machinery for human education which must pass away like

Heb. x. 1,
cf. ix. 11.
Cf. 1 Cor.
xiii. 11.

childish things. Much about it, therefore, was destroyed by being fulfilled. As the shell breaks when the bird is hatched; as the sheath withers when the bud bursts into leaf; as the rough sketch is done with when the picture is finished; as the toys of boyhood are laid by in adolescence; as, in short, whatever is only preparatory is evanescent, and perishes in the hour of maturity: so it was inevitable, that whatever portions of the old economy were educational and introductory, should fall off when the Fulfiller came. This destruction of outer form accompanies every unfolding of truth. Nothing lives and abides save that eternal Word of God, Who is the personal and perfect utterance of God Himself; every word of man in which for a time this Word of God is more or less fully uttered, like every flower of grass in which a little of the divine may be discerned, must wither and pass. It is a thing never to be overlooked, that truth is more than any form or expression of truth we know. God is greater than His own revelation of Himself. As the conceptions of men regarding the Father and His relations to the world in His Son, have grown stronger and clearer, so have they found for themselves new vehicles of utterance and new symbols to reflect them. Truth

PART I.

GENERAL PRINCIPLE.

1 Pet. i. 24, 25.

PART I.
GENERAL
PRINCIPLE.

may have many modes of exhibition; each of them it shivers in succession, as a healthy oak-shoot the pot which holds it. Shaking must follow shaking, till all that is of the earth be shaken off; then shall remain only that which cannot be shaken. Men's thoughts change and widen; but He abides, Who is God's perfect Word, 'the same yesterday, and to-day, and for ever.' In Himself, Christ Jesus gathers up every broken light of truth, each 'jot or tittle' of true goodness, which ever found expression in decalogue words or verse of prophet, or in any verse or word of any man; and in Him they find their just place and supreme fulfilment: for in Him are hid all these treasures of wisdom and knowledge.

Heb. xii. 27.

Heb. xiii. 8.

Col. ii. 3.

This great word of the seventeenth verse is not to be read in any sense narrower than the widest which it will bear. It is as true of the prophets as of the law, that Jesus was not their destroyer, but their fulfiller. It is true of all antecedent systems and doctrines which had in them the least soul of goodness or of truth, no less than of Mosaism, that the Son of God came to 'fulfil.' For, in fact, it belongs to the divine nature as discovered to us in His character, that He hath no love to destroy. God aims ever at fostering what is good, unfolding what is involved, ripening what is immature. Throughout physical processes, as in the rearing of spiritual manhood, we trace the Divine Hand at this loving task; making the most of everything, educing good out of ill, causing life to grow from the ashes of dead life, and finding in each lower or evanescent form of existence a step by which to rise to something nobler. Is not this characteristic of His working, Whose presence we detect throughout the universe, that, where He comes, He comes not to destroy, but to fulfil. But although, as His manner was, our great Teacher dropped a word so wide and endless in its truth as this word must be taken to be, yet its immediate application was narrowed in the next following sentence to the Mosaic law, and especially to its ethical element. Jesus was about to lay down the moral duties of citizens in His heavenly kingdom; and what He was at present concerned to show, was that His new code of duty was not destructive of the traditional Hebrew code, but a fulfilment of it. The law of Moses was to the Jews whom He addressed the highest expression which they knew of the eternal righteousness of Jehovah as a rule for man's behaviour. Were these commandments to be broken or destroyed by the legislation of the new

PART I.

GENERAL PRINCIPLE.

Vers. 18-20.

kingdom? Jesus answers, at this point, as at every point: 'No, not broken, but kept; not destroyed, but fulfilled!'

The illustrations which Jesus goes on to accumulate in the rest of this chapter, five in number, will give us ample opportunity to examine His mode of dealing with the Hebrew law. But before we descend to any of these particulars, this seems the place to try if we can gather His general principle of treatment.

The moral law of Israel, both as summarized in the decalogue, and as amplified by many minute statutes in Exodus and Deuteronomy, was a law not of principles so much as of instances: that is, it abstained as a rule from classifying actions under wide ethical categories, and contented itself with specifying particular acts. It forbade individual sins; it commanded individual duties. In its form it was a code of details, of prescriptions for external conduct. It would lead me too far aside to ask how this external form of the law was rendered needful by its educational purpose, on the one hand, as a 'pedagogue' to conduct the race to Christ; or, on the other, by the fact that it was less a guide to personal virtue than the statute-book of a civil society, the public law of a commonwealth. I only note the fact

Marginalia:
PART I. GENERAL PRINCIPLE.
Ex. xx. 2-17.
Ex. xx.-xxiii.
Deut. xxi.-xxv.
Gal. iii. 24, Greek.

that it did prohibit this and that offence, prescribe this and that behaviour, and prohibited far more than it prescribed. All the while, the single deep-lying principle of evil in the human heart, from which every form of wrong-doing takes its rise, as well as the one supreme condition of the heart which is the spring of virtues, were left almost unnoticed.[1] Selfishness in the heart was that which made each transgression of law to be a sin; love, what made an act of obedience to be a virtue. But of love and selfishness the law had little to say. The real principles of action, which in the last resort make a right act to be right, and a wrong act wrong, lay beneath the surface of a statute book which bristled in every paragraph with Thou-shalts and Thou-shalt-nots. However explicable such a phenomenon may be when we know its reason, and its adaptation to the wants of the Hebrews, it was plainly an imperfection, one of those defects which called for fulfilment. It even constituted a snare for shallow natures; it almost tempted people into a pharisaic righteousness. The outward letter of the law could be so easily kept; and the law was nearly all outward

PART I.

GENERAL PRINCIPLE.

---

[1] Not altogether; as such passages as our Lord (in Matt. xxii. 37-40, and parallel passages) cites from Lev. xix. 18, Deut. vi. 5, and x. 12, suffice to show.

PART I.
GENERAL
PRINCIPLE.

letter. How could weak and tempted men, with undeveloped consciences, be expected to read beneath the words of the decalogue, or be harder on themselves than God appeared to be, or see that a law was not really kept in any sufficient sense when its terms were formally observed, and its spirit secretly defied? It is true that in rude times, a law which stayed the hand of violence and shut the mouth of perjury might do much to keep society sweet; but it could hardly go very far towards teaching rude men the evil of malice or the beauty of truth. Nay, statutes of this sort actually proved to be the occasion of a pernicious distinction betwixt righteousness and goodness. If it was possible for a bad man to keep within the terms of a statute, the eternal distinction between goodness and badness would seem rather to be obscured than insisted on. Besides, the chance that a law is long observed depends on the absence of any general desire to break it; a decalogue, therefore, which could not stanch evil passion at its source proved a weak embankment against its overflow. So it came to pass, that in all later and worse times of Hebrew history, men's ideas of righteousness retreated within those mere rules of ceremonial which anybody could keep, and the bare prohibition against acts of murder, or theft, or adultery, proved no restraint at all on violence, knavery, and lewdness.

It is plain that laws of this sort never could be 'fulfilled,' that is, filled full with their own proper meaning and force, till some one should draw forth to light the spiritual, far-reaching principle of morals which underlay them, and should show men that in that, not in the outward letter, lay their real ethical value as a transcript of God's own character. To draw out of each its moral principle, and then to run all these moral principles up into one royal law of love, was much. To postulate such a royal law in the heart, and then run it down through the details of life and show how it would secure the fulfilment, not only of each 'jot and tittle' of commanded duty, but of ten thousand duties, which no statute book could specify; this was more. Something like this, other men besides and before Jesus had in substance attempted. Hebrew prophets and heathen philosophers had alike discovered that virtue is not so much the observance of a code, as the living growth of a loving heart. One thing immeasurably greater remained to be done, essayed by neither philosopher nor prophet: to exhibit in practice a complete fulfilment of all laws through the possession of perfect love, and

B

PART I.
GENERAL
PRINCIPLE.

plant such love in others' hearts, that they too shall live out righteous lives in obedience to no prescriptions, but under the natural impulses of a regenerated nature. To expound the law is less than to keep it; to keep it, less perhaps than give others power to keep it too. In all three ways is Jesus the only Fulfiller and 'the

Rom. x. 4. end of the law.'.

To separate Jesus the moral teacher, from Jesus the example and the saviour, of men, is to misunderstand Him. If, as He sits and expounds His nation's laws upon the hill, you see in Him no more than a master of duty, a Hebrew moralist more advanced than Moses, more spiritual than Solomon, more practical than Isaiah; you will utterly fail to understand the power which this Sermon on the Mount has wielded. To tell us, as He does, that the spirit of even the decalogue lies in a right love for God, and a love for all men, like God's own love for them, and that therefore the Old Testament code itself is fit, when you understand it, to become a new code for the kingdom of God, will not go far of itself to make our world a good world. No; but add

Phil. ii. 6-8. only this, that the Speaker is God Himself under His own law, fulfilling in the guise of a servant the duties which He lays on us. This divine

King is King because He is the first of subjects, and Himself pays absolute respect to His own statutes. He is a Jew, circumcised to keep the whole law. He is more—the Son of God, Whose accepted business it is to fulfil all righteousness. So He walks in all outward ordinances of Mosaism blameless; with an observance of each 'jot and tittle' of ceremonial and civil duty more irreproachable than scribe or Pharisee. Yet how infinitely His righteousness exceeds the standard of the most punctilious! To Him the divine law is a copy of His Father's character; and obedience to law is just a son's tribute of love to his father. Rising, therefore, from the letter of law to the mind of the paternal Lawgiver, this Son kept the commandments in their spiritual meaning, obeyed with the freedom of choice, and served in the spontaneity of love. He Himself it was Who practically translated the old legislation into the new, Who so fulfilled the letter as to turn it into spirit, and Who, while faithful to 'carnal ordinances,' liberated the principle of righteousness, which is love, from its fleshly envelope, and made it the principle of a new kingdom of God. His own life is the meeting-point of two economies; the practical fulfilment of the Old Testament, its practical elevation into

PART I.

GENERAL PRINCIPLE.

Cf. Luke ii. 49; c. Matt. iii. 15.

PART I.
___
GENERAL
PRINCIPLE.
Isa. xlii. 21.
Matt. v. 48.

a New Testament. The law was never so entirely 'magnified' as when God's Son showed that, to keep it as it ought to be kept, meant to be perfect as God is perfect; and by so keeping it, realized in manhood the perfection of the Godhead.

By expounding its spirit, Jesus fulfilled the law in its inherent and everlasting force as a law of heart and motive.

By keeping the law in spirit as well as letter to its last fibre of obligation, Jesus fulfilled it as a condition of divine favour and everlasting life.

By enabling His brethren to love the heavenly Father Who gave it, Jesus fulfils it as the rule of life in all believing men.

'I am not come to destroy, but to fulfil.'

FIRST ILLUSTRATION:

THE SIXTH COMMANDMENT.

Ye have heard that it was said by them of old time, ' Thou shalt not kill; and, whosoever shall kill shall be in danger of the judgment:' but I say unto you, That whosoever is angry with his brother without a cause shall be in danger of the judgment; and whosoever shall say to his brother, ' Raca,' shall be in danger of the council; but whosoever shall say, ' Thou fool,' shall be in danger of hell-fire. Therefore, if thou bring thy gift to the altar, and there rememberest that thy brother hath aught against thee; leave there thy gift before the altar, and go thy way; first be reconciled to thy brother, and then come and offer thy gift. Agree with thine adversary quickly, whiles thou art in the way with him; lest at any time thy adversary deliver thee to the judge, and the judge deliver thee to the officer, and thou be cast into prison. Verily I say unto thee, Thou shalt by no means come out thence till thou hast paid the uttermost farthing.—MATT. V. 21–26.

THE SIXTH COMMANDMENT.

I PROCEED to consider the first of those five examples by which our Lord at once defines and illustrates the relation of His New Testament legislation to that of the Hebrews. That relation, as we have seen, is not destruction, but fulfilment. The moral law of Moses, like every other part of the Old Testament system, held in germ the perfect law of Christian ethics; but it enclosed that germ within a temporary envelope of external civil statutes. The work of the Fulfiller must therefore be to search for the spirit of the law beneath its details, and to set free from the mere letter of it those moral principles on which it rested. In doing this, Jesus struck at two errors, which, though opposed, did equally 'break these commandments, and taught men to break them:' the error of popular antinomianism; and the error of pharisaic legality.

PART I.
FIRST ILLUSTRATION

Cf. ver. 19.

The sixth commandment of the decalogue, as graven by God's finger on the granite of Horeb, stood in the brief and pungent style of that code

Ex. xx. 13.

PART I.

FIRST ILLUSTRATION

thus: 'Thou shalt not kill.' If you approach this prohibition in the temper of a jurist, who sees no more in it than a law for the protection of society against criminal violence to the person, you will not find it a hard command to keep. Hold your hand from bloodshed, and you are within the law. This juristic style of interpretation, however, will not bear to be carried into the province of morals. Read the word of God defining human duty as you would a police regulation, and instantly you create a false morality; you breed self-righteous moralists. If what God forbids on this branch of conduct is no more than such acts of violence as can be dealt with by the sentence of a court of justice; then we may feel very safe and righteous, who never lifted our hand to slay, and may be as severe as we please on our unhappy brother who has lifted his. Such was the line of interpretation adopted by the Jewish expositors, who appended to the sixth commandment the rider quoted by our Lord. Addressing the people, who, in an age of few books, were indebted for their knowledge of Scripture to the public reading of it with rabbinical glosses in the synagogue, He said : 'Ye have heard that it was said by [or to] them of old time, Thou shalt not kill; and whosoever shall kill shall be in danger of the judgment;' that is, shall be liable to the jurisdiction of the local bench of magistrates, who in each Jewish town had the power of capital punishment.

But you may approach the sixth commandment in another spirit, and find a very different interpretation possible. Let it be viewed as embodying a moral principle for the regulation of the individual life; let conscience face it in an earnest and religious mood, to find out what it has to tell of God's character, and how He would order the relation of man to his fellow-man: then the words will be felt to cover by implication far more than meets the ear. Morality is an affair, not of overt act, but of motive. The judgment of God searches the heart; and the earnest or devout interpreter will ask, in front of a law like this, What is that state of the criminal which makes killing a crime? No Jew could help seeing that the mere act of taking life was not always murder. The Mosaic system even recognised the old *vendetta*, or feud-vengeance,—swift, red-handed retaliation by a next-of-kin,—though it laboured to moderate the barbarism of that custom. The voice of God certainly had sealed with express sanction every writ for the legal execution of criminals; and the law punished a num-

PART I.

FIRST ILLUSTRATION

Ex. xxi. 12-14; c. Josh. xx.

ber of crimes with death. All Hebrew history, moreover, viewed Jehovah as sustaining the cause of justice in the last ordeal of battle, fighting as the Lord of Hosts and the Captain of a people armed in a righteous quarrel. Nay, the law did in so many words exempt from blame accidental homicides; and the ground on which it did so made it as clear as terms could make it, where the guilt of killing lay. It said, 'Whoso killeth his neighbour ignorantly' is 'not worthy of death, inasmuch as he hated him not in time past.' Not the blow, therefore, but the hatred, was the sin of the sixth commandment, even as a civil statute. Killing, on the principles of Mosaic teaching, might be no murder. It might be blameless; it was often righteous; sometimes it was even praiseworthy. When justice armed the executioner or the warrior, bloodshed became his duty. But hateful passion prompting the fierce and sudden blow, or still more, fed into a grudge in the heart —this was the sin against God and God's image in man which made manslaughter to be a crime, and filled with moral force the bald hard word, 'Thou shalt not kill.' Nor was this a mere inference from the law. For, in fact, the Pentateuch offered to one's hand its own key, when it bore upon its pages words like these: 'Thou shalt not hate thy brother in thine heart. . . . Thou shalt not avenge nor bear any grudge against the children of thy people; but thou shalt love thy neighbour as thyself.' I quote these words from Leviticus, in order to show that our Lord neither made a new law nor put a new sense upon an old one, when, to the superficial juristic reading of the scribes, He opposed a more spiritual interpretation. The fact is, that the pharisaic reading could only have been hit on by men of shallow nature and cold hearts, in a time when formalism had slain morality; whereas the deeper exegesis of Jesus was actually suggested in the Mosaic books themselves, was involved in the whole prophetic period of the Old Testament, and had been recognised by earnest and honest Hebrews in every age. The one was in reality the destruction of the commandment, the other its fulfilment.

Our Lord was not content to set aside the flimsy rider which later tradition had attached to the sixth commandment, and to fall back on that older and more scriptural interpretation which read in it a condemnation of hatred and unjust anger. He did more. He tracked this sinful passion from its concealed presence in the heart, onward to the confines of murderous act. To each degree He affixed a deepening penalty;

Part I.

First Illustration

Lev. xix. 17, 18.

PART I.
FIRST ILLUSTRATION

but to mark how far the divine outruns in its severity all human justice, He attached to the lowest grade of passion the same supreme sentence which human jurisprudence reserves for the highest.

Three grades of guilt short of murder in the breach of this sixth commandment are instanced by our Lord: causeless anger, provocation to hasty speech, and deliberate insult. There are three degrees of penalty to correspond, borrowed from Hebrew jurisprudence: the judgment, the council, and Gehenna. But the lowest degree of judgment meted out to suppressed anger is the same as in rabbinical procedure formed the penalty of murder. By so much is heavenly justice in God's new kingdom stricter and more exigent than Hebrew law. A little elucidation of the text will be needful to bring this out. First let me try to explain the three degrees of guilt. The first is:

Whosoever is angry with his brother without a cause.—As all killing is not murder, so all anger is not hatred. It is even one mark of a noble and pure nature, to be susceptible of that just and honest anger which is the recoil of the generous against the base, of the true man against the liar, of the chaste against the lewd, of all manly virtue against villany and shameless outrage. Even when it is the injured person himself in whose cheek this passion flames, it may be quite noble; for oppression can turn even weak women and cowardly men for the time into moral heroes. Much more when high-spirited men resent the wrong done to others; or better still, the wrong which every injury inflicted by the strong upon the weak does to the majesty of justice, and to Him Who is the avenger of the right. It would be well for us if at this hour in England we had more of that public indignation which makes each citizen the guardian of his fellow, which represses the cruelty of domestic and social tyrants by the civil sword, and which, when it strikes at criminals, strikes not for the advantage of society only, but as well for righteousness and for God. In such indignation there is no hatred. It is clear from malign breath, as the steel sword of justice. It is at its core charitable, for it springs from the love of the good; and against the bad it bears no ill-will, but a most tender and pure pity.

From it stands as far removed the causeless anger in which all breach of the sixth commandment begins, as darkness stands apart from light, or love from hate. It matters little whether this

PART I.

FIRST ILLUSTRATION

word rendered 'without a cause' stand part of the original text, or is (as it may be) a gloss suffered to creep in at a very early date.[1] In either case, it carries the sense of the passage in it. Guilty anger is guilty, because it is not moved by an adequate ground in the conduct of the offender; finds no sufficient moral justification for itself; and draws its warmth, therefore, not from the justice of the case, but from personal passion. Such anger as a man is stung into by his neighbour's misconduct, not because right is wronged or God offended, but because his own interest or feelings have suffered: this is anger without cause. It is blind, because it will not look at the justice of the case. It is vindictive, for it is a personal wound which has to be atoned for. It is hasty, for it is heated and cannot pause to grow cool. It is spiteful, bent on returning evil for evil. It is the mother of hatred and the first secret fount of murderous violence. Who of us does not know by frequent experience what it is to be provoked by some sudden wrong, or the crossing

---

[1] It has against it the authority of the Vatican and Sinaitic manuscripts, as well as of some old versions, and is rejected by Tischendorf, Lachmann, Meyer, and (though on internal grounds only) Tholuck. If a corruption, it must have found its way into the text within the second century.

of our pleasure, into this heedless, bitter, hot-hearted temper, which forgets itself, and loses sight alike of mercy and of fairness? Who has not felt its restless, fiery workings? Whoso, saith Jesus, is thus angry with his brother, has broken already the sixth commandment.

The second degree is thus expressed:

Whosoever shall say to his brother, 'Raca.'— 'Raca' was a slight colloquial exclamation, used by the Jews when annoyed or irritated. It probably meant nothing, and therefore cannot be translated; or if it had originally some slang meaning of contempt, it had ceased to suggest its first idea, and was muttered by the provoked or ill-tempered man without thinking what it signified. It is thus a specimen of a class of angry expletives, common enough in all languages, which serve as what may be called a safety valve or harmless outlet for irritated feeling. But irritated feeling ought to be denied all outlet. Ill-nature which is kept under control by the restraint of principle or one's better feelings, is not so bad as ill-nature which finds vent in a word, even in a word so slight and meaningless as this; ay, though we mumble it through our clenched teeth. Our Lord therefore sets His mark upon such discharges of irritation, as not only bred by a passionate and spiteful heart, but as betraying a lack of control, a passion which breaks, though no more than breaks, into utterance; a thing worse for us, and for our neighbour, than to endure the pent-up throes of unjust provocation in one's own breast.

There is a still worse stage:

Whosoever shall say, 'Thou fool.' — In the Palestine vocabulary of abuse, this word meant a great deal more than the last. It conveyed, when used in passion, a charge of senselessness and wickedness at once; and was the bitterest epithet ill-will could compass when in full explosion.[1] As 'Raca' marks the lowest stage of spoken displeasure, where anger just passes into half-involuntary scolding; so 'Fool' seems here to mark the last stage, when anger is on the point of passing beyond speech into intemperate act. No man could permit himself to address his brother

---

[1] I need hardly say that of course the word might be used, and innocently used, where no utterance of temper was involved at all. As an expression of just indignation, our Lord Himself applied this, with still harder terms, to the pharisaic party (Matt. xxiii. 17; cf. ver. 33 and Luke xiii. 32). With sorrowful earnestness, He addressed it to His two disciples at Emmaus (Luke xxiv. 25). Apostles were not afraid to follow so high an example. (Gal. iii. 1; Jas. ii. 20). But it is Quaker-like childishness to press the outward letter of the Lord Jesus, where the spirit in which the word is used is so opposite. This is to be, in spite of all His teaching, New Testament Pharisees.

man in a deliberate term of serious insult who had not lost all self-command; unless, indeed, habitual explosions of temper had made the employment of abusive speech easy to him. When self-respect, justice, and kindly feeling are all trampled in this way under the hoof of animal rage, what is left, save cowardice, to hold back the hand from a blow? Our Lord has tracked the evil temper from its beginnings in unjustifiable resentment to the very verge of that open violence at which even pharisaic morality, like our public justice, was compelled to deal with it.

To each stage in this ascending breach of the sixth commandment our blessed Lord has attached a penalty. There is no satisfactory way of reading these penalties, save to understand them as implying degrees in God's punishment of sin, but degrees of an unknown divine penalty expressed in terms borrowed from the criminal jurisprudence of the Jews. Two of the words used are certainly so borrowed. 'The Judgment' was the title of a local or municipal bench of justices, which sat in every little town of over one hundred and twenty of a population, and had the power to sentence criminals to death by beheading with the sword. 'The Council' is a common name for the supreme court of the Sanhedrim,

C

which sat in Jerusalem, had exclusive cognizance of the gravest offences, as treason or blasphemy, and could sentence to death by stoning. The third word is the 'Gehenna of fire,' which cannot here mean, as it sometimes did, the place of final woe, for that would be a most inconsequent third to two Jewish forms of civil trial. The verse becomes intelligible when we simply read 'Gehenna,' not as a type for hell, but in its own proper sense, as the name of that terrible and ill-omened ravine of Tophet in the valley of the Sons of Hinnom just under Mount Zion, which for so many a Hebrew age had been held accursed; which from the times of the evil kings, who there burnt hideous sacrifices of infant life to Moloch, down to the day when Judas went to it to hang himself, had been a receptacle for the foulest refuse of the city; where, too, were sometimes flung, after their execution, the unburied bodies of the worst criminals; where (in Isaiah's awful words) the worm never died, and the fire was never quenched. It may be true that murderers were never cast out after death to lie unburied in that foul dell; as little were they stoned by the Sanhedrim; but none the less did these words of Jesus mark to Jewish ears an ascending series of shame and horror in the punishment of the criminal, till the last aggravation known to Jewish law or practice should be reached. It was impossible that these three modes of capital punishment could be taken literally. No Jewish tribunal could deal with that heart-anger with which He began His series; angry words could not be so punished by earthly judges; no such division of jurisdiction in cases of violence was known to Hebrew usage. The three graduated modes of execution are simply borrowed as images of those unknown penalties which await the prisoners of divine justice beyond this life; and the stern lesson of the passage concentrates itself in this thought, that at the Almighty's awful bar, and before His face Who searches hearts, the secret indulgence of unlawful malicious anger counts as murder does in earthly courts. Higher degrees of sin in respect to temper there are, and for higher sin God reserves a higher penalty: but so infinitely more rigorous is the moral code of the new than of the old kingdom, that where Israel's civil jurisprudence ended, the spiritual penalties of God begin; and the lowest grade of what He calls murderous passion runs parallel in His eye to that supreme act of violence which men call murder. It is by this law of the new kingdom we must be tried. In two directions it exceeds in severity the civil

> PART I.
> FIRST ILLUSTRATION

law of commonwealths. First, it judges all unjustifiable irritation, however slightly expressed; nay, even when it is not expressed at all. It goes down into the bosom of every angry man, and sentences him for his unrighteous anger. Next, for the passionate heart or hasty word, it has a penalty as much more terrible than civil death, as spiritual and eternal penalties transcend those which are temporal. We are bound to a righteousness which is inward, spiritual, intensely moral; and we are bound to it by penalties which are of the world to come. Surely this law is not destroyed; it is fulfilled.

Who of us can keep this law? Searched by a test so penetrating as this, there is no conscience clear. We are all at times too hasty, short of temper, or unreasonably provoked. We all do vex one another by irritability; we now and then wrong one another by causeless ill-will. Every one of us, therefore, has cause to be thankful to Jesus that He added to His law words of hope, to tell us how, when we have broken the sixth commandment, we may still escape the judgment of Heaven. The last four verses of the passage are a long but most needful appendix, which in two separate forms sets forth one lesson.

The angry man, who is angry without cause, and in his anger has spoken rash and wounding words or offered open slight, has wronged his brother. It may be that the offended brother complains of the wrong before God or men; it may be he does not: no matter. In either case, the angry man has made an adversary of the Most High. God is the Avenger of the wronged; and the object of your injurious displeasure or your abusive speech is under the shield of the Almighty. Punishment waits for you at His bar, to be averted only by confession at His altar now. But before confession at the altar of divine mercy can save you from sentence at the divine bar at last, the confession must be made, not to God only, but to your injured brother; reconciliation must be won with man first, and then with Heaven. This single lesson, which an apostle summed up afterwards in these words, 'Confess your faults one to another, and pray one for another, that ye may be healed,' is illustrated twice over by our Lord in a vivid popular form. The first scene turns on the altar of mercy; the second on the bar of judgment: the first is a drama; the second a parable.

A Jewish worshipper is already in the temple court, waiting till his turn comes for the officiating priest to present his sacrifice to Jehovah. As

PART I.

FIRST ILLUSTRATION

1 Thess. iv. 6.

Jas. v. 16.

Vers. 23, 24.

he stands before God to confess his faults and ask for mercy, there naturally rises into memory an unacknowledged breach of this sixth commandment. By some angry word or injurious deed he has wronged his neighbour. What shall he do? He is in act to sacrifice, about sacred duty, offering propitiation to offended God; yet there is an earlier and more urgent duty. Worship can better wait than reconciliation. Apology and restitution are sweeter offerings to God than a lamb, for they are the sacrifices of a broken and a contrite heart. Nay more; worship is vitiated, sacrifice is refused, prayer and incense are abomination, so long as the offender is unreconciled to the offended. 'Go, then, on the instant; stand not on ceremony, but leave thy gift, and go: first be reconciled by becoming acknowledgment, and, if need be, by reparation, to thy brother; then, with a clear conscience and a tearful but lightened spirit of sweet and lowly penitence, return to offer, in all joyful confidence, thy gift of atonement, with confession and with prayer, to the no longer averted face of the Eternal Judge.'

A child can read that lesson; and the proudest of men are they who need it most. But because there are those who never go to God's altar, and would never be reminded by their baffled

[margin: PART I. FIRST ILLUSTRATION; Ps. li. 17.; Cf. Isa. i. 11-17.]

search for reconciliation to the Father that they needed first a brother's pardon, Jesus puts the same lesson into more urgent and alarming words. All men do not approach God's footstool of grace; but all men know that they are drawing near to God's seat of justice. The imagery now is from a civil action at law, where a plaintiff sues a defendant for a debt. The road of life is for all of us a road with a tribunal at the end of it; and he who travels towards his grave in company with fellow-men whom he has hated, miscalled, or aggrieved, against whom he has been angry without reason, is like a debtor who walks side by side with his creditor on their way to court. A few steps further, and both parties will have passed into that awful judgment hall together — into the place where already the Judge of all the earth sits and waits for us. Well did these Galilean peasants who heard Jesus, know that once they carried their petty disputes before the stern Sadducean face of a local justice, their chance of compromise or private composition was over. It was good advice for a debtor to agree with the plaintiff while they were on the road, and to do it quickly; lest, if the creditor handed him over to the court, the judge should commit the insolvent to the officer, and the officer to gaol. But the

PART I.

FIRST ILLUSTRATION

Vers. 25, 26.

words of the Preacher swell and grow weighty with an infinitely more solemn and awful significance, when He adds, with His usual trumpet-note of warning: 'Verily I say unto thee, Thou shalt by no means come out thence till thou hast paid the uttermost farthing.'

In this species of debt to one another we are all insolvent. No brother may have formally lodged complaint against us in the supreme court, or appealed for justice against our violence and wrath. But there is One Who undertakes every cause; and with Him, not with our brethren, we have in the last resort to do. Who of us can say, before His face, that we were never angry without a cause, have never vexed a heart by peevish passion, nor ever spoken the words that bite, nor nursed a dark, malignant, envious, or hateful temper within our breast? Who of us goes clean-handed to be tried by Christ's version of the sixth commandment? And shall we risk by obduracy the sentence of that Judge? Are we in wrong against any man, and dare we travel, impenitent and unpardoned, towards death? Think: your brother dead, past hearing of your too late repentance! or you dead, snatched unshriven from his presence! Ah, let no man live his uncertain days in an unreconciled feud! All along the road of life there is possible for us a continual confessing and atoning and reconciling, a making up of differences, and apologizing for wrongs, and healing of hurts; and with that mightier Plaintiff behind, he who has won his brother's pardon may also be reconciled at the altar of Immanuel's sacrifice. A few more steps only; and we may stand before a bar where there is no forgiveness and from which there can be no appeal!

SECOND ILLUSTRATION:

THE SEVENTH COMMANDMENT.

Ye have heard that it was said by them of old time, 'Thou shalt not commit adultery:' but I say unto you, That whosoever looketh on a woman to lust after her, hath committed adultery with her already in his heart. And if thine eye offend thee, pluck it out, and cast it from thee: for it is profitable for thee that one of thy members should perish, and not that thy whole body should be cast into hell. And if thy right hand offend thee, cut it off, and cast it from thee: for it is profitable for thee that one of thy members should perish, and not that thy whole body should be cast into hell. It hath been said, 'Whosoever shall put away his wife, let him give her a writing of divorcement:' but I say unto you, That whosoever shall put away his wife, saving for the cause of fornication, causeth her to commit adultery: and whosoever shall marry her that is divorced committeth adultery.—MATT. V. 27–32. Cf. MATT. XIX. 3–9, and parallels; also XVIII. 8, 9, and parallels; LUKE XVI. 18.

THE SEVENTH COMMANDMENT.

<small>PART L
SECOND ILLUSTRATION</small>

OUR Lord's first example to show that His relation to the law of Moses was fulfilment, not destruction, was the sixth commandment of the decalogue; His next is the seventh. The former was the law of temper, regulating offences between men; this is the law of marriage, regulating the relation of the sexes.

Our Lord cites this law precisely as it stands in the original Mosaic code. It was not needful to quote any pharisaic gloss, because it was now evident that they would read these words, as they had read the words of the sixth, literally. To their literal understanding of the words, 'Thou shalt not commit adultery,' our Lord is content briefly to oppose a deeper interpretation. Exactly as, in the former case, He had gone back from the act of killing to the passion of unjust anger, in which killing takes its rise; so here He goes back from the act of adultery to the unlawful lust which is its cause. The marriage law differs, indeed, from the law against malicious anger in this, that it places a restraint which may be called arbitrary upon a natural appetite. There is an anger also which is righteous as well as an anger which is wicked; only in this case the distinction lies in the very nature of the anger itself, and would have been felt by the untutored conscience apart from external statutes: whereas it is the express ordinance of God which makes sexual love within the marriage bond a lawful and pure thing, and outside the marriage bond a sinful and defiling thing. It is true that this primeval ordinance has its roots very deep in the constitution of the race. For, first of all, God created the two sexes so, and so balanced their numbers, that each filled out and made up the complement of the other, with this evident design, that one man and one woman should be in everything the helps and counterparts of one another, and by their union realize the perfect condition of human life. Besides, God placed the appetites of the body under the control of reason and of the higher social affections; so that a man feels himself degraded if his love for a woman is more animal than moral in its character; that is, if the higher elements in it are subordinated to the baser. These two facts in the human constitution—the complementary relation of the sexes, and the preponderance of moral and social affections over brute instinct—are facts which lie at the basis of marriage: they make chastity, that great virtue and beauty of character which is not possible for other creatures, whether above us or below us, possible for men; they form the preparation which God the Creator laid for the marriage ordinance of God the Legislator. Still, the marriage ordinance sets a fence round about the relations of the sexes which is in a sense arbitrary, because it rests immediately on the command of God. The command is primeval. It dates from Eden. It has survived, not the fall only, but the dispersion, the migrations, the disintegrations, the embrutement, of the races of men. It has undergone almost endless corruptions. It has had to tolerate polygamy, concubinage, polyandry, lax divorce, the acquisition of wives by violence or barter, the holding of them as chattels, the use of them as slaves. Among barbarous tribes and in rude ages, all these and other abuses have modified or overlaid the blessed marriage law; but they have not cancelled it. In the worst cases, marriage has somehow and in some shape survived; and upon the passions of the most savage and debased it has always imposed a certain check.

Now, wherein lies the essence of this marriage

PART I.

SECOND ILLUSTRATION

PART I.
SECOND
ILLUSTRATION

law? It aims at keeping the relation of man and woman pure, by permitting intimacy only within a given guarded bond betwixt one man and one woman. But these relations are not kept pure by merely controlling the outward behaviour of the sexes to each other. The relation of man to woman is a relation of inward feeling, of passion; and unless the marriage law can control the desires and passions of the sexes, it fails to secure purity. Therefore our Lord reads the seventh commandment as virtually a commandment for the government of the heart. He distinguishes, in fact, three stages in the breach of it. The first and outermost is that which the law expresses: adultery. From this consummated breach of the marriage bond, He goes back upon the earliest voluntary expression of criminal desire. That earliest voluntary expression is, the gaze. For, when He says, 'to look on a woman to lust,' He does not mean any involuntary excitation of passion through a casual sight or presence of its object. It is through the eye primarily that passion enters; but if the eye be turned away, and the moral purity of the heart expel the intruding movement toward sin, then the law is not broken; on the contrary, it is kept. It is when the criminal impulse is so far indulged that the eye is purposely directed to rest with pleasure on the exciting object, that the earliest act of unchastity is committed. Even this is not yet the beginning of adultery. To look at a woman in order to lust after her is the earliest bodily manifestation of the sin; yet it is not so much the perpetration of the crime, as the first proof that a man has perpetrated it. Before that look, there came the inward indulgence of desire; the consent to a forbidden appetite; the surrender of the soul's pure and loyal protest against unlawful relations. 'Already,' therefore, says our Lord, tracking the sin inward now to its real seat, 'already the man has committed adultery in his heart;' for he has submitted his will, and, with his will, one at least of his members, to the dictation of an unhallowed desire. Henceforth it is occasion, or impunity, and not desire, which fails him; it is not the consent of his will, but something else, which hinders the prosecution of the crime into adulterous act.

Beneath a law so scrutinizing, so subtly penetrative, which expects our loyalty for the sanctities of marriage to be so scrupulous, which demands that the soul's purity shall repel the very first approach of prohibited desire, and calls the briefest impure glance a crime,—beneath such a law, who shall say there is any one chaste? Dare any of us have the secret history of his heart ransacked? This moralist on the mount is to be our Judge. How shall we answer Him for the imaginations which have defiled our private hours, for the prurience to which we gave house-room, for the warmth of look, the desire which dared not betray itself by a gesture? The purest-minded of youths or maidens may fitly suffer these words of Jesus to bear upon the conscience, in order to warn each one against the insidious approaches even from afar of dishonourable and unhallowed affection. There is no one who does not need to dread its entrance into those secret recesses of the nature which ought to be the home or shrine for God's most pure Spirit.

To His brief exposition of the spirituality of God's law on this delicate subject, our Lord subjoins virtually two appendices.

The first appendix runs parallel to the practical exhortation appended in the preceding case of the sixth commandment. In that case He bade the man who had given his neighbour offence by hasty wrath, leave the holiest duties of religion on one side until he had cleared the way for God's forgiveness by 'first being recon-

Marginalia:
PART I.
SECOND ILLUSTRATION
Cf. 1 Cor. vi. 18, 19.
Vers. 29, 30.

ciled to his brother.' To repair the wrong of angry passion by at once apologizing for it, was a natural lesson to be learnt from the law against murder. Till the innocent sufferer by injurious anger has been pacified, nothing is done. The sin of unchastity is not less exigent. To rid oneself of it, is quite as pressing as to repair a wrong. Only, in its early stages, it is not another who is injured by it; it is the spiritual nature of the sinner himself which suffers most. 'Every [other] sin,' as St. Paul explains, 'that a man doeth is without the body; but he that committeth fornication sinneth against his own body.' The evil is already done when impurity is suffered to rest for an instant in the heart; for then the heart and inward nature of the man is defiled. When impurity passes into act, when it directs one movement of the hand, or so much as a glance of the eye, the body also is debased from its legitimate functions and prostituted to unholiness. For a sin which so instantly and fearfully avenges itself upon the doer of it, in soul and body, no *ex post facto* atonement provides any remedy. A man cannot apologize to himself for the lewd imagination which has for one permitted moment turned his soul into a sty. He cannot make up by subse-

PART I.

SECOND ILLUSTRATION

1 Cor. vi. 18.

Cf. Tit. i. 15.

quent confession for the debasement his own nature has suffered. Remedies after the act do not avail here. Prevention is the only cure. Hence all moralists have prescribed for those who are tempted to this sin, not resistance, but flight. 'Flee fornication,' says St. Paul. Job made a covenant with his eyes. 'Remove thy way far off,' said Solomon, 'and come not nigh.' So the wise son of Sirach: 'Gaze not,' ... 'look not round about thee in the streets,' ... 'turn away thine eyes.' It is in the same line that this Divine Teacher insists on the most ruthless self-denial and mortifying of fleshly appetite, as the only way for the passion-tempted and endangered soul to escape defilement. On another occasion Jesus used these same vehement images —the amputation of our most useful member, the right hand; and the excision of the most pleasant, our right eye—to express in a more general sense the stern and painful need under which men lie to sacrifice everything to the avoidance of any sin. Here there is a peculiar propriety in them. The particular sin referred to is a sin of the body. The ordinary and innocent enjoyment of bodily pleasures is that very line along which danger to chastity meets the young and hot-blooded. It is pleasant to see pleasant and fair society, but there is a certain society into which a young man cannot enter without perilous excitement. There is a class of books which, though some may, others cannot, read without catching a stain from fascinating but doubtful passages or indelicate innuendoes. There are objects of art which to the pure indeed are pure, but on which some eyes cannot look without a suggestion of impropriety. What then? Let no man judge his fellow's freedom, or erect his own evil mind into a censor upon the good of better men. On the other hand, let no man trifle with his own safety, or try how he can touch pitch and keep his fingers clean. To restrict one's pleasures and pursuits to the limit which is safe, will mean self-denial. It will entail effort. It may be a loss of advantages which others can reap without harm. It may even prove to be such self-inflicted martyrdom as that buffeting and bruising of the body, for the sake of mastering it, of which St. Paul wrote to the licentious Corinthians. No matter. Better a thousand times to forego all use and joy of sight or touch; better to have neither eye to see with nor hand to toy with; than be decoyed by loose glances and soft touches into that habit of impurity which entangles a man, body and soul, in

PART I.

SECOND ILLUSTRATION

1 Cor. x. 29.

Cf. Isa. lii. 11; quoted in 2 Cor. vi. 17.

1 Cor. ix. 25–27.

PART I.
SECOND
ILLUSTRATION

such meshes of lust as no Samson can break through, which drags the self-despising, despicable victim of his own indulgence down that road of deepening abomination which ends in the hell of the licentious, the foulest circle in the whole Inferno.

Not, of course, that any literal violence, such as earnest but misguided men have now and then practised upon their bodies, can touch the seat of this moral plague. Surgical modes of cure would not be too painful, nor the disfigurement of amputation too shameful, could they only purchase that purity which is the life of the soul. But the virus of lust, sharper and more deadly than any poison, works too deep for surgery. When all foreseen occasions or provocatives to sin have been manfully cut away, and every care taken not to rouse the evil which slumbers in the heart, there will still remain the real battle of conscience and reason and modesty against appetite; a battle to be fought at last within the secret soul of each tempted man, and for which help is to be found nowhere but on one's knees. To forego pleasures which other people call innocent, to tear yourself from the gayest company, to impose on yourself the sharpest fasts or self-displeasing, would be a cheap *recipe* for the eradication of this sin, were it only an effectual one. Yet despise not these outward helps and conditions to a cure, if you are in earnest for purity. Call not this asceticism; if it is, it is the asceticism which is rational and Christian. Everything is right, and not right only, but needful, which will cut off the occasion of images that are unclean, and desires that are beyond control. Our Master is no Puritan, but He is the most thorough and the most severe of all moralists.

<small>PART I.

SECOND ILLUSTRATION</small>

The second appendix to our Lord's brief exposition of the law of marriage bears upon divorce. It looks at the first glance like a fresh example of how Jesus fulfils in His new kingdom the law of the old; for it opens with a similar formula: 'It hath been said,' and it opposes to the traditional divorce law of the Jewish scribes a regulation which might be called original. The law regulating divorce, however, must be, from the nature of the case, a corollary from the great law of matrimony, when rightly understood; and therefore I read it as simply an appendix to the teaching of the twenty-eighth verse. Jesus' attitude to the divorce customs of His time forms a curious chapter, sufficiently large and difficult to deserve handling by itself. The question came before Him more explicitly on a later occa-

<small>Vers. 31, 32.</small>

sion, when it received at His hands a fuller treatment. Here I can only resume His teaching on the point as it bears upon those views of the marriage tie which are here in hand.

Moses found the original law on marriage considerably relaxed, and a practice prevalent which permitted the husband to dismiss his wives on almost any pretext. The reasons for so loose a usage run back, through the Egyptian servitude, to the polygamy of patriarchal times and the relation of rich sheiks to their slave concubines. At any rate, the liberty of divorce was one which, at the giving of the law, it was not possible or prudent to abolish. Legislation sought to reduce its licence by sundry restrictions. Thus, divorce was by Moses prohibited, except for some discovered 'fault of uncleanness,' as the phrase went; and even then was not to be legal unless registered in a formal written document. The divorced parties, moreover, could not re-marry with one another. Had these rules been honestly kept, the discreditable laxity springing out of polygamy would have been modified into something like a tolerable system for a civilised commonwealth. But at this point again came in the wretched system of juristic quibbling. The phrase 'matter of uncleanness' was elastic as well as obscure, and the lawyers stretched it to cover the most frivolous pretences. One school of Jewish doctors in Jesus' time [1] had come to teach that a trifling neglect of household duty, immodesty in dress, or even the arbitrary preference of a capricious husband, formed ground enough for dissolving the marriage tie. Of course, no sanctity could attach to a union which, on such slender pretexts, could be legally broken; and against this scandal the great Teacher of Galilee sternly opposed Himself. But Jesus went much further. Instead of making the Mosaic legislation His basis, He went back upon the original meaning of wedlock as a primitive ordinance of God. Founding on the words of God at the creation of Eve, as recorded in the earliest document of revelation, Jesus taught that, in the purpose of the Creator, the two sexes were made for each other; that each mutually completed the other's deficiencies, so that both together made up the ideal of humanity; that the holy bond of matrimony was the recognition of this fact in human nature; and that it effected a perfect union between one man and one woman, a union so sacred as to be inviolable, so perfect as to be permanent, a union which left them, in fact, no

PART I.

SECOND ILLUSTRATION

Gen. ii. 24; quoted Matt. xix. 4–6.

---

[1] The school of Hillel.

longer two, but one flesh. Starting from this most blessed and sacred thought of the Almighty in the first creation of male and female,— a thought which must always lie at the very base of society, of home, and of all social and domestic sanctities,— our Lord inferred the inseparableness of the marriage tie. He declared the Mosaic law of divorce to have been merely a temporary and unavoidable lowering of the original standard, an exceptional concession to special circumstances. 'For the hardness of their hearts,' He said; because a more rigorous enforcement of the bond would only have exasperated a rude, untrained people, and made the evils worse which it was meant to mend. Since such facilities for divorce were not the true law of matrimony, but a regrettable limitation of it, they behoved to fall away when the final and perfected economy came, of a Christian kingdom, in which the great Fulfiller interprets the divine will in its integrity, and enables His subjects to keep it in its spirit. Clad with divine authority to republish the law of God, Jesus proclaimed, as the guarantee of wedded rights and the sanction of wedded duty within His Christian kingdom, this principle: 'What God hath joined together, let not man put asunder.'

The solitary exception which He allowed, is an exception in appearance rather than in reality. For if the union of the two sexes into one flesh forms the essential characteristic of marriage, then adultery is not so much a reason for dissolving that union, as the virtual dissolution of it by the formation of another. It lies in the nature of the case, that a tie which is by anything else indissoluble, is by the mere fact of unfaithfulness dissolved.

No apology is required for setting in as clear a light as possible the lessons of the Lord Jesus on this subject. Our Lord never spoke more explicitly on anything than He did on this; on no subject is it of greater moment for the well-being of society that His deep words should be revered and understood. The social state of any people will be found ultimately to hinge on the purity of its homes and the place which it gives to woman. The jealous separation of the sexes in Asia, leading to brutality in indulgence and to indelicacy in reserve; the unmentionable vices of classical Greece; the exaggerated worship of celibacy in debased Christianity, with its painful reactions from the fourth century to the present; these examples teach how much depends on sound popular conceptions of the relation between the sexes. If one were asked to name that branch of public morals on which the teaching of Jesus has wrought the most wholesome reformation, this should be the one. Whatever modern Protestant Europe knows of household peace and the sanctities and confidences of home life; whatever consecrates the hearth into an altar, makes a Bethel of the house, or gives to manhood a chivalrous loyalty and to woman pure-heartedness with innocent freedom,— all that we owe to the precious words of this stainless Man of Nazareth. It was His teaching on the marriage law which first cut down by their roots the widespread abuses of concubinage and polygamy; which elevated chastity to the front rank among virtues; which exposed the essential criminality of every unhallowed breath; which raised woman to her rightful place, and secured her respect and liberty by throwing around her the shield of love. If for any one thing, in the present condition of English society, we have reason for the devout thankfulness which has in it no evil pride, it is for this, that in England home is a sacred place. It is for young men before all others to keep it so. Let them learn the pure and manly lessons of Jesus Christ. Let them reverence their own bodies as the temples of God. Let them fear to lower, even by a look or word, the fence which God's hand has reared around the honourable and holy estate. Let them shrink from no severity to chasten, and control, and subdue themselves. Above all, let them seek the moral strength and love for the pure which come through vital union to the Lord Jesus Christ. Let them wear, not on their breast, but in their heart, the red cross of that blessed Son of Man, the whitest of the sons of men: so shall they conquer the flesh, and emulate in a nobler contest the purest and manfullest of the knights of old;[1] so shall they attain to walk with Christ in the white armour of an unsoiled and guileless character. Into His eternal city of transparency 'there shall in nowise enter anything that defileth, neither whatsoever worketh abomination.' May He blanch us all into perfect chastity, and preserve in us blamelessness of heart and life!

PART I.

SECOND ILLUSTRATION

Rev. xxi. 27; cf. xiv. 4.

---

[1] Cf. Tennyson's 'Sir Galahad' (*Poems*), and his treatment of the same legend in *The Holy Grail*.

THIRD ILLUSTRATION:

OF OATHS.

Again, ye have heard that it hath been said by them of old time, ' Thou shalt not forswear thyself, but shalt perform unto the Lord thine oaths.' But I say unto you, Swear not at all; neither by heaven, for it is God's throne; nor by the earth, for it is His footstool; neither by Jerusalem, for it is the city of the great King. Neither shalt thou swear by thy head, because thou canst not make one hair white or black. But let your communication be, ' Yea, yea;' 'nay, nay:' for whatsoever is more than these cometh of evil.—MATT. V. 33–37. Cf. MATT. XXIII. 16–22.

OF OATHS.

IN two examples we have already seen how Jesus' teaching fulfils the Jewish law. In His third instance, which is the law against perjury, He does not quote, as in both the former, from the decalogue; for false swearing is a compound sin, breaking at once two of the ten commandments. It is, for one thing, an act of profanity, in breach of the third commandment: 'Thou shalt not take the name of the Lord thy God in vain;' it is also an extreme act of false witness, in breach of the ninth: 'Thou shalt not bear false witness against thy neighbour.' Of course, it does not exhaust by any means the breach of either commandment; for there is much profanity on the one side, and much lying on the other, which do not take the form of an oath. Perjury lies at the point where these two sins overlap one another: it includes the guilt of both. We are accustomed, in a loose use of words, to apply the terms 'oath' and 'swearing' to very many forms of profane language besides

*Part I.
Third Illustration*

Ex. xx. 7.

Ver. 16.

perjury; we apply them popularly to curses, to blasphemy, to ribald exclamations, to the use of over-strong epithets, and so forth. It is therefore important to make it clear what the swearing of an oath strictly and properly means.

It is, to begin with, a form of witness-bearing. Every man who states what he means to be taken for a fact is a witness. He bears testimony to something which he professes to know, and which his hearer is supposed not to know. His statement is either a true testimony to his own knowledge and belief of the fact, or it is not. Behind all such witness-bearing—that is, behind every word which a man affirms with the intention of being believed—there is to be understood one other Witness, always present, Who sees everything, Who knows what I know, hears what I say, and judges whether what I say be true to what I know. This heart-searching Witness, 'the faithful and true,' is the final Judge of appeal betwixt him who testifies and those to whom the testimony is borne. His unbounded knowledge and absolute veracity form the ultimate test of human truthfulness. He is the supreme defender or vindicator of the true—supreme avenger of the false. If I am true, His infallible testimony will in the end corroborate

Of Oaths.

and justify, however my testimony may be now contradicted by false witnesses, or enfeebled by suspicious appearances. If I am false, however I may win credit for the time, my lie must in the end be shattered before the manifestation of His avenging truth. Always, therefore, when men speak in seriousness to a fact, there is this awful background to be understood. There is One Who knows, and Who will one day declare, the truth. Always, men speak under correction of the Omniscient. But when the speaker expressly recalls to his own and his hearer's remembrance this tacit appeal; when he calls in as corroborative testimony the invisible and infallible Witness; when he solemnly invites the testing judgment of Almighty God to attest his own suspected veracity, then he swears an oath. To swear truly is to bear honest witness, and back it with the sanction of a religious invocation. To swear falsely is to lie, and profanely to endorse the lie with the awful name of the most true God; it is to make the authority of the Almighty and men's fear of His judgment vouchers to gain belief for falsehood.

The prohibition of this compound sin Jesus found in these words of the national statute-book: 'Ye shall not swear by My name falsely,' which *Lev. xix. 12.*

PART I.
THIRD ILLUSTRATION

PART I.

THIRD ILLUSTRATION

He quotes briefly thus, 'Thou shalt not forswear thyself.' To this, which is all that stands in Leviticus, He appends the rider of the Jewish doctors. One would have thought it difficult to evade by any gloss the force of a law so explicit; the ingenuity of Hebrew casuistry accomplished it. In another book of the Pentateuch, there was found a statute on the subject of vows, which ran thus: 'If a man vow a vow unto the Lord, or swear an oath to bind his soul with a bond, he shall not break his word.' This is a more limited law than the former. It refers to one class of oaths only—oaths which vowed some voluntary religious service to Jehovah. But the jurists applied this narrower statute to limit their interpretation of the more general one; and then read the larger law against perjury, as if it ran thus: 'Thou shalt not forswear thyself, but shalt perform to the Lord thine oaths.' The 'but' is emphatic; for the latter clause is meant to circumscribe the former: only the breach of oaths to perform some religious service is to be reckoned perjury. The words 'to Jehovah' are also emphatic; for if the oath is not made expressly by His sacred and mysterious name, to break it is counted no forswearing. Thus, at last, in the hands of quibbling and unscrupulous pedants,

Num. xxx. 2; cf. Deut. xxiii. 21.

God's broad prohibition of false oaths of every class dwindled into this surprising shape: 'That which thou hast expressly sworn by Jehovah's name to do unto Jehovah, that thou shalt perform on pain of perjury, and no more.' Well might the indignant voice of Jesus declare that a statute-book which had been wrested out of shape and emptied of moral meaning by such casuistry as this, had been 'made of none effect by their tradition.'

<small>PART I.
THIRD ILLUSTRATION</small>

<small>Matt. xv. 6.</small>

Of course, teaching of this sort bore wretched fruit. Since no oath was thought binding unless made in the express name of Jehovah, a crowd of minced oaths grew into practice, which came near that sacred name without actually pronouncing it. Lies, backed with these sham oaths, bred a system of wholesale and almost sanctioned perjury in common life. The intercourse of man with man lost all regard to truth, when the holiest safeguards of truth were habitually travestied or defied; and the people sank, as the Bedawîn of the present day have sunk, into a 'nation of universal liars.'[1] Profanity, too, kept pace with falsehood. If an oath was no guarantee for truth, but the accepted garnishing for a flat untruth, what sanctity could attach to any words?

---

[1] Thomson, *The Land and the Book* (Lond. 1859), p. 383.

> PART I.
> THIRD
> ILLUSTRATION

Liberal indulgence in the frivolous or profane use of sacred things and names could hardly be blamed, so long as they kept clear of that one unmentionable Name, round which it seemed that all sacredness had superstitiously gathered itself. At that day, therefore, as to this day, in Syria, the reckless incessant abuse of the most awful words was probably next to universal in common speech. 'No people,' says Dr. Thomson, 'that I have ever known can compare with these Orientals for profaneness in the use of the names and attributes of God. The evil habit seems inveterate and universal.'[1] Long before Christ's day, a Hebrew moralist had found it

> Ecclus. xxiii. 9-13.

needful to say, with all emphasis, 'Accustom not thy mouth to swearing, neither use thyself to the naming of the Holy One. . . . There is a word that is clothed about with death: God grant that it be not found in the heritage of Jacob.'

It was not enough, however, to censure, as others had done, the false morality which bore such profane fruit. Our Lord fulfilled the law by disclosing those principles which deeply underlay it.

The perfect idea of human speech is, that

---

[1] *Ut supra*, p. 191.

simple assertion and simple denial have in witness-bearing the force of an oath. If both the speaker and the hearer were, as God is, perfect lovers of the truth, and if the speaker always spoke, as he ought to speak, in the presence and under fear of the all-knowing Witness; then everything beyond the bare words 'It is,' or 'It is not,' would be superfluous. A perfectly truthful witness obviously needs no oath to bind him. He is always 'on his honour,' and 'tells the truth as he shall answer to God at the great day of judgment.' For the present, indeed, this ideal state is so utterly and hopelessly an ideal, that the whole practice of social and juristic language must proceed on another assumption. Each man, according to his experience of human nature, will fix for himself the extent to which he believes what he hears, or the kind of asseveration which he will demand as a pledge of veracity. I fear most men get incredulous as they get older, and make a larger and larger discount on their neighbour's language for wilful or unconscious falsehood. At any rate, society has to guard itself against the lie by every safeguard, where public interests are involved. The cumbrous phraseology of the law, its system of witnesses, registrations, oaths, and deeds, its penalties for perjury and forgery, are

PART I.

THIRD ILLUSTRATION

only so many testimonies to the ruin of human honour, and the facility with which men lie at the bidding of cupidity and of fear. But it is the work of Jesus Christ to recall humanity to its ideal, and in His church to educate men at least towards the perfected condition. The condition in which oaths shall be needless, and speech be perfect with a 'Yea,' 'Nay,' is at least an approachable condition, even if it is not under existing circumstances an attainable one. In general society, or in business, as in the commonwealth, it may not be always possible to dispense with the oath; but within the church or select society of men who have learnt the truth as it is in Jesus, it ought to be quite possible. Within the church, therefore, or new spiritual kingdom, and between men who address each other as fellow-subjects of Jesus Christ, the old law, 'Do not forswear thyself,' has been superseded by the deeper law, 'Do not swear.' Thus, at a single stroke, Jesus sweeps away from His inner realm of purified hearts, along with the whole system of strong language, those modes of paltering with truth by which men have always tried to give their neighbour a guarantee for veracity, and yet to deceive him. Evasive or minced protestations, white falsehoods, prevarications, concealments which affect to conceal nothing, roundabout and double phrases, all shabby cloaks in which falsehood hides its nakedness, and the winding, underhand tricks of speech by which words are made to hide or to pervert thought,—all these flee away before the face of an honest man; and in their room He bids us put a plain, straightforward, earnest 'Yes' and 'No.' One round unvarnished truth routs a host of cowardly falsehoods. It is an unspeakable advantage for the world, that here, in the midst of our smooth conventions, our impudent puffs of trade, our sneaking fibs, our big and windy asseverations by which bluster tries to win credit for a lie, there stands now continually this King of Truth. In this true Israel, unlike His first ancestor who wore the name, there is no guile. His open, frank, sincere eye is a rebuke to the world's duplicity. Before the world, which barely believes in truth at all, He holds up from age to age the noble and severe ideal of an earth in which each man shall utter, and each man shall believe, the very truth, and nothing but the truth. To those who name Him as their Lord, and who, banded in His name, profess to exhibit some faint forecast of what this earth shall be when all men own His sway, He gives but this most plain word to keep among them-

PART I.

THIRD ILLUSTRATION

Gen. xxxii. 28; cf. John i. 47.

selves and before the world: 'Let your commucation be, "Yea, yea," "Nay, nay."'

The secret of such veracity as Jesus thus requires in His kingdom,—such veracity, I mean, as makes an oath needless, because it reckons its 'yea' to have the force of an oath,—lies in the abiding fear of God. What a witness who swears gives me as a guarantee for his truthfulness is, that he expressly invokes the presence and judgment of Almighty God. That is to say, he gives me just such assurance as his faith in God and fear of Him when in most intense exercise can give, be it much or little. The measure in which the swearer feels religious reverence is the measure in which I can trust his oath. Now, suppose a man to stand always consciously in the presence and beneath the eye of God, and to have habitually upon his mind that reverential apprehension of the Almighty which the swearer summons up for the moment; is it not evident that such a man's naked word is of the very essence and nature of an oath? If, with his lips in words, the true man never needs to pledge his religious dread of the Almighty Detector and Punisher of falsehood, it is because in his heart he is always speaking under that tacit dread of Jehovah. The state of religious reverence which makes swearing solemn and gives it value is the state in which a Christian ought habitually to be. Hence, the more you bring people into a condition of mind to feel the sanction of an oath and to dread false swearing, the nearer you come to abolishing oaths altogether. This new law of Christ: 'Let "Yea," "Nay," be like an oath,' is just the supreme fulfilment in its spirit of the old law: 'Do not perjure thyself.'

PART I.

THIRD ILLUSTRATION

It is further to be observed, that the same religious reverence for God which so effectually cures false witness that it abolishes all need for serious oaths, cures also the profanity of frivolous swearing. We saw at the outset how the sin of perjury embraces both falsehood and profanity. The falsehood Jesus condemns in its roots, by making every word as sacred as an oath. The profanity He tracks through every minced or meaningless utterance of sacred words. People who have no reverence for God have often a superstitious dread, like the Jews, for His name; and when they use a flippant or insincere oath, they cajole their conscience by putting in its stead some word which sounds less holy. Such people care only for the husk of the law, and welcome any subterfuge which will let them break it in its spirit, while they keep its letter.

PART I.
THIRD
ILLUSTRATION

They shun to 'take the name of God in vain;' but they will profane anything in His heaven or earth without compunction, and coin new, puerile, or unmeaning oaths, for the mere pleasure of being profane. Of such oaths Jesus gives examples to illustrate two different classes.

In the first, the swearer substitutes for the divine name something more or less connected with God, which stands, at first at least, as His representative. Of this class are the current Hebrew oaths cited by our Lord—by heaven, earth, or Jerusalem; the current English oath—'by heaven;' Roman Catholic oaths by the cross, and the saints, and the angels, and the Virgin; and more remotely those modern oaths, which have the distinction of being stupid as well as profane—'by Jupiter,' and the like. For it has been reserved for us moderns since the Renaissance to make our irreverence contemptible, by substituting divinities we do not believe in, for Him whom we still call our God, yet choose circuitously to insult. In this last case, the thing sworn by has no sacredness, for it has no existence. But wherever a man swears by anything he does revere, the oath is really by the Eternal Himself; for all venerable things are venerable only through their connection with Him. Heaven is sacred, says Jesus, quoting from the splendid page of Isaiah, for it is His throne; and earth, because it is His footstool; saints, because they are His holy ones; and the temple, because He dwells in it. To a heathen who saw in the breeze and the forest, the stream and the sun, symbols or shrines of a separate indwelling divinity, these natural objects were truly divine, and fit to be sworn by. The Greek who swore by them, heathen as he was, swore devoutly. For us, there is no less sanctity about each part of God's earth and heaven because we see in each not a local and secondary deity, but Him Who 'filleth all in all,' Who speaks in thunder, and rides upon the cloud, Who bids the sun to know its rising, and counts the number of the stars. Let us fill our hearts with reverence for the everywhere present Father, as His glory has filled the earth; and we shall find nothing common or unclean enough to be the subject of an idle or irreverent oath.

<small>PART I.
THIRD ILLUSTRATION
Isa. lxvi. 1.</small>

<small>Eph. i. 23.
Ps. xxix., civ. 3;
Isa. xix. 1;
Job ix. 7;
Ps. cxlvii. 4.</small>

Perverted oaths of the second class are of the nature of imprecations. In every oath the swearer exposes himself, in case of falsehood, to divine judgment. But instead of exposing himself, he may devote to judgment some minor forfeit, something of his own which he puts, as it were, in pawn to attest his veracity. This is the

PART I.
THIRD
ILLUSTRATION

character of the last Hebrew oath quoted by our Lord: 'Neither shalt thou swear by thy head;' as when men swear by their honour, kings by their crown, soldiers by their sword; or when people stake their life, their soul, or some such dearest thing, in pledge of sincerity. However thoughtless protestations of this sort may be, the underlying reference always is to God: for as it is He Who alone can decide on our veracity, so it is He alone Who can dispose of what is thus rashly submitted to His decision. If the forfeit of a false word is to be one's head, or soul, or credit; who is the lord of these, to take them or confirm them, but God? No man can 'make one hair of his own head white or black.' And the man who fears God as God ought to be feared, will have too profound a sense of God's sovereignty, and too awful an apprehension of God's judgments, to imprecate his Maker's intervention either to sustain a lie or to decide a bagatelle. There is, in fact, no cure for either false or flippant swearing, but devout reverence for God. Fear God, and you will fear to lie. Fear God, and you will count each serious word sacred as an oath. Fear God, and you will feel that there is no oath but one; since all swearing, however diluted or whitewashed, runs up into an appeal to the Almighty and Omniscient. Fear God, and you will think twice before you let slip a random adjuration or a rash imprecation: for every oath must be, if irreverent or needless, a profanity; if false, a perjury. Therefore 'swear not at all.'

We are now, I think, in a position to judge how far our Lord's teaching forbids all administering and taking of oaths whatsoever. It cannot surprise us that many have drawn that conclusion from such sweeping words as are here employed. We associate the refusal to take a judicial or allegiance oath with Quakerism; but in fact there has rarely been absent in any age of the church a small section of Christians who held this ground, and numbers of the best fathers of christian learning have spoken strongly in its favour. Moreover, it is unfair to deny that our Lord does set it before His church as the true ideal of His kingdom, that veracity and trust among His followers should make everything beyond 'yes' and 'no' superfluous, and because superfluous, wrong. That christian heart which does not beat quicker at the thought of such a golden future, of such a realm of truth kept through the fear of God, has little sympathy with Christ. Yet such a superseding of oaths can only come from within, through

PART I.

THIRD ILLUSTRATION

So Chrysostom, Theophylact, Jerome, and others.

the spiritual elevation of men at large into truthfulness and trustworthiness; not at all by any external prohibition. To forbid oaths by arbitrary edict, before you have made men honest enough to be able to do without them, would be to gain nothing. To keep such an edict in the letter of it, would be to repeat the Hebrew fault of legalism, even though the edict issued from the lips of Christ. Christ trusts us to understand Him so well, that we shall care as little as He cares for any mechanical observance of His own rules, but shall care as much as He cares to see them kept by the inward inspiration of the Spirit. The New Testament is full of evidence that even within the Christian Church the time had not yet come for the abolition of oaths as superfluities. Jesus Himself responded to a solemn judicial adjuration by the high priest in council, when He would respond to nothing else. St. Paul in various passages thought fit to use both the full form of oath: 'I call God as a witness upon my soul,' and abbreviated phrases which meant the same thing. One of the latest acts of revelation is to record the awful oath of the angel who announced that time should be no longer. Nor can these cases appear strange to any man who recalls with such solemn thankfulness as befits the occasion, how it has pleased the Eternal Truth, the 'I Am,' to stoop to our weakness of faith, and, because He could swear by no greater, to put His own existence in mysterious pledge for the confirmation of the promises of His grace to mortal men; in order that His awful oath might put an end to all strife of doubt and alarm within our sinful hearts, and bring to us 'strong consolation,' and a hope made doubly sure by 'two immutable things.' If ever a bare word ought to have been enough, Jehovah's ought. Through our sin of suspicion, it was not: and Jehovah sware. A man's bare word ought always to be enough. Through our sin of lying, and the distrust which lying has bred, it is not: and true men on fit occasions may swear. For in truth, as we have seen, all witness-bearing by a true man is tacitly done under a solemn sense of the highest sanctions; and when he swears, he only expressly states for others' security what that is which—oath or no oath—has bound him always to speak the truth. Still, 'it cometh of the evil.' Sadly as well as solemnly will a thoughtful man swear; for to make such a concession to the dishonesty and incredulity of mankind, as to assert in what awful presence, beneath what judging eye, I bear my witness to the

PART I.

THIRD ILLUSTRATION

See Gen. xxii. 16, quoted in Heb. vi. 13ff.

Ver. 37, Greek.

truth, is to testify the humiliation of my kind. Yet is it to be done frankly and fearlessly when need is. It would be but a vain stickling at a word were we to sacrifice truth itself, and certitude, and justice, and the very ends of witness-bearing and of speech, to a superstitious dread of saying out like men what all the while we hide reverently in our hearts, that God is our witness before Whom we stand. Verbal Quakerism is but Pharisaism over again. 'In understanding' let us 'be men.'

'Howbeit,' in falsehood as well as malice, let us 'be children.' The mean and cowardly sin of wilful unveracity infects the society, and especially the trade, of England, to an extent which some tell us grows from year to year, and threatens to rob us of what was wont to be an Englishman's boast among the nations. One does not need to be a prophet, to see that as the living faith in a personal Deity, before Whom we shall be judged, and by Whom we shall be punished, decays (for it seems to be decaying) out of the heart of our people, the best safeguard for truthfulness will decay. When one knows that, alongside of this decay of the fear of the living God, the reasons for seeking gain, and the pressure of business competition, and the facilities for knavery in trade, are all increasing round about us; how is it possible to look forward without a fear lest the word of an Englishman may come to be as little trusted as any word spoken on the exchange? It is for Christians to set their faces like a flint against all the current forms of false witness; to prize and guard the perfect fair form of truth. Let them be for their own part transparent as the floor of heaven; and when occasion offers, let them expose, and scorn, and flout the baseness of every imposture.

FOURTH ILLUSTRATION:

LEX TALIONIS.

Ye have heard that it hath been said, 'An eye for an eye, and a tooth for a tooth:' but I say unto you, That ye resist not evil: but whosoever shall smite thee on thy right cheek, turn to him the other also. And if any man will sue thee at the law, and take away thy coat, let him have thy cloak also. And whosoever shall compel thee to go a mile, go with him twain. Give to him that asketh thee; and from him that would borrow of thee, turn not thou away.—MATT. V. 38–42.

But I say unto you which hear, . . . Unto him that smiteth thee on the one cheek, offer also the other; and him that taketh away thy cloak, forbid not to take thy coat also. Give to every man that asketh of thee; and of him that taketh away thy goods, ask them not again.—LUKE VI. 27–30.

LEX TALIONIS.

THE three illustrations of Christ's relation to Hebrew law which we have hitherto considered, were of a different character from the two last which we now approach. The laws against injurious anger, against lust, and against perjury, are merely prohibitory laws. They forbid distinct acts of crime; and although Jesus has taught us that they cannot be kept by simply avoiding overt acts, but must have a root of obedience in the heart, it is, after all, only a negative species of virtue which does no more than keep the passions under control, and the conversation truthful. To the positive side of christian ethics our Lord now turns; and in the two instances we have still to consider, He pushes His demand for positive beneficence or brotherly love to the loftiest and most divine extreme.

Here, as before, however, this new moralist attaches His precepts to earlier legislation. He still appears as the Fulfiller of the old; correcting the narrow and unkindly interpretations

PART I.
FOURTH ILLUSTRATION

PART I.
FOURTH ILLUSTRATION

which Jewish casuistry had put upon the primitive text, and reading beneath its lines deeper principles of virtue than they had been able to detect. Both the instances which He selects are limitations which had been unduly put upon the duty of mutual kindness betwixt man and man. In the first, a principle of public jurisprudence had been supposed to arrest the operations of private charity. In the second, a spirit of national or selfish particularism had been suffered to narrow its range. Both restrictions are by Jesus' larger love swept away. For injuries we are to return, not judgment, but mercy; while the objects of our charity are to be, not some men, but all men.

The verses we have now before us correct and read backwards a misused principle of public law —the so-called *jus talionis*.

The criminal code which God gave to the free Hebrew people fully recognised the principle of equivalent retaliation. It enacted as follows: 'If a man cause a blemish in his neighbour, as he hath done, so shall it be done to him; breach for breach, eye for eye, tooth for tooth.' Nay, it went further in the later recension of it: 'If a false witness rise up against any man to testify

Lev. xxiv. 19, 20.

Deut. xix. 16–21; cf. Ex. xxi. 22 ff.

against him that which is wrong, ... then shall ye do unto him as he had thought to have done unto his brother, ... and thine eye shall not pity; life for life, eye for eye, tooth for tooth, hand for hand, foot for foot.'

It must be carefully remembered—what the Jewish lawyers forgot, and their forgetting it explains their whole blunder—that this statute was part of the criminal code of a commonwealth, and had for its end the satisfaction of public justice. It was no rule for private revenge. It put no licence to retaliate into the hand of any private person. The law of the state only, acting for public ends of justice and through its own officers, exacted this stern retribution. Nor did the law exact this *quid pro quo* for the sake or advantage of the injured party, but solely for the vindication of justice. When one man injures another in person, estate, or reputation, there is, of course, a claim to recompense in the shape of damages or *solatium* to the plaintiff. This our English law allows, and this the Hebrew law allowed. Such civil damages the Old Testament knows under the name of 'restitution.' For theft, for accidental fire-raising, for trespass on private grounds, for the loss of borrowed goods, and other descriptions of injury, Hebrew law awarded restitution,

PART I.

FOURTH ILLUSTRATION

Cf. Ex. xxii. 1–15.

which was to be of equal value, or double, or fourfold, or even fivefold, according to the case. But the *jus talionis*, or principle of retaliation, which I have cited, is quite different. It belongs not to civil, but to criminal law. It deals with misdemeanours, not injuries. It awards, not damages, but punishment; and therefore (which is the vital point) it is a rule, not for private plaintiffs, but for the public prosecutor. The mistake of the Pharisees' interpretation, which our Lord combated, was a very gross one. They read the criminal law of the realm as if it had been a moral rule binding on the individual conscience. Because the law held an aggressor liable to suffer a loss equivalent to that which he had inflicted, therefore they thought every injured person might lawfully desire and claim a like retaliation. This was simply to legalize the *vendetta*, the oriental blood-feud. It was nothing less than the elevation of revenge into a right, if not into a duty.

Such a perversion of moral principles could find no favour from Christ. But it does not follow that, because He censured the transference of retaliation to private life, therefore He meant to censure its application to criminal jurisprudence. I suspect that, in point of fact, the right of retaliation lies at the basis of all sound criminal jurisprudence. It is plain enough, of course, that to carry out such a right, as Mosaic law did, with literal harshness,—maiming a prisoner, for example, in the member which his violence had maimed,—was possible only in a barbarous or a very simple state of society. This was but the grim expression then found for that rude sense of retributive justice which lay in the hearts of men. In the awards of more advanced ages, as in our Lord's day, some proportional commutation of loss or suffering, in the form of fine, imprisonment, exile, or hard labour, has always been substituted for the literal 'eye for eye,' and 'stripe for stripe.' It ought unquestionably to be added, that those more humane laws, which have been dictated by the christian spirit to modern christian nations, have aimed (with what success it is not for me to say) at other ends rather than at punishment in the strict sense. At present, criminal legislation seeks, and rightly seeks, partly to reform the criminal, and partly to deter others from crime. But I am not at all sure that we do well to make these the exclusive designs of punishment, so that punishment shall only be felt to be justified when it secures, or at least tries to secure, one or both of these ends; that, in other words, we are on safe ground when we strip civil justice of that more awful and godlike prerogative of retribution which was once its most dreaded sanction. The supreme Magistrate of the universe has planted His own white throne upon this primitive axiom of equity: 'As he hath done, so shall it be done to him.' It seems to me that in every human heart He has embedded an ineffaceable sense of the fitness, that is, of the justice, of this rule. When it shall come to the last judgment on all of us, we are taught in the Sacred Book, as well as by natural conscience, that God will pay sinners back according to their sin, and make each man reap as he has sown. It is a rude way, but it is a way, of putting the same thing, to say: 'An eye for an eye, and a tooth for a tooth.' To make this principle of retaliation, therefore, a basis for our treatment of public criminals, is at least to rest ourselves on the very base of the divine dealing with transgressors of His spiritual laws. If it should be thought that this is venturing too far into the most delicate and awful privileges of the last great Judge, let it be remembered that 'the powers that be are ordained' by Him, that they do not bear in vain the sword with which He hath girt them, and that they are His ministers

Marginalia:
PART I.
FOURTH ILLUSTRATION
Lev. xxiv. 19; cf. Matt. vii. 2.
Rom. xii. 19, citing Deut. vii. 10, xxxii. 35; Gal. vi. 7; cf. Rom. ii. 6 ff.
Rom. xiii. 1–6.

for this very end, 'to execute wrath on him that doeth evil.' To me it seems clearly enough taught in Scripture, that to magistrates there has been delegated a limited portion of this most sacred and solemn function of judgment for the avenging of wrong and the vindication of right, not simply for ends of correction or prevention. Were state government an arbitrary device of men, drawing its sole sanction from the voluntary concurrence of the community and aiming solely at mutual protection, one could understand how its penalties might have no better justification than this, that they tended to keep person and property safe from individual passion. But if the state is, according to the older and, as I think, biblical view, a divine institute; if magisterial authority is lent of God; if He must always be felt as the unseen King by Whom kings reign, the ultimate and real Sovereign of every realm, then each earthly throne and seat of judgment may well repose upon no meaner stay than the same stern maxim of just recompense on which stands His own; and His vicegerents, clothed about with a more awful majesty than man could give, may have something to do even with this supreme function of justice, with discharging upon the criminal, all consequences apart, the naked vengeance of outraged law. When the judge speaks, and the officer of law strikes, they strike and speak, not in the name of the people, but in the name of God, Who is the King of kings.

In such retaliation, however, there is no hatred. As God punishes without malice, in a just wrath, which is free from personal irritation, and forms only the shadow-side of His love; so His civil ministers, who execute justice, ought to be too impartial and unimpassioned for any revenge to stain the purity of their ermine. It is quite otherwise with private and individual retaliation. Men cannot be trusted to do justice in their own quarrel, for personal retaliation generally means spite. When Jewish moralists taught that the injured might claim eye for eye from the aggressor, they found no support in the Old Testament. The same statute-book which had said, 'Eye for eye,' said also: 'Thou shalt not avenge nor bear any grudge against the children of thy people.' This was also the teaching at a later day of the royal proverb-maker: 'Say not thou, "I will recompense evil;"' 'Say not, "I will do so to him as he hath done to me."' It was therefore no new commandment which our Lord opposed to the legalized revenge of His contemporaries, when He forbade them to resist evil;

but a primitive Mosaic principle of morals which He only rescued from neglect and set afresh in the forefront of social duty. His words, 'Resist not evil,' contrast curiously with the terms of an apostolic command, 'Resist the devil;' and the contrast helps us, I think, to understand them both. The Evil One and all evil ones are certainly to be strenuously withstood by every honest man, when he can in any wise hinder by his resistance their doing of evil. So long as evil to ourselves or others is only intended or on the way of being inflicted, so long is the time for resistance, 'striving,' as one says, 'even unto blood.' But once the evil act has been done, further resistance becomes no longer self-defence, but vengeance. Deeds done are in God's keeping. To strive that evil should not be wrought is no more than loyalty to God, Whose soldiers we are in this war: but it is soldiers we are to be, not executioners; and when no other end can be served by opposition but repayment of evil on the evil-doer and vengeful requital, private men may not usurp His prerogative Who hath said: 'Vengeance is mine; I will repay.' To forget this, is to open the door for unlimited indulgence in mean spite, unjust contention, endless feuds, and all uncharitableness.

PART I.

FOURTH ILLUSTRATION

Jas. iv. 7.

Heb. xii. 4.

Rom. xii. 19.

PART I.

FOURTH ILLUSTRATION

So far, then, I understand Jesus to do no more than correct a current misuse made of the Mosaic criminal law, by opposing to it a forgotten principle of Mosaic morals. This, however, is far from exhausting His reading of human duty. To restrain the hand from returning a blow is negative virtue. Jesus adds, on the other hand: 'But I say unto you.' What He says unto us is

1 Cor. xii. 31.

the 'more excellent way' of a diviner love. It is a new and backward reading of the misread *lex talionis*. 'Resist not evil; but whosoever shall smite thee on thy right cheek, turn to him the other also.' These will always be strange words. When He spoke them, they were very novel words. They were spoken by the Son of a heavenly Father, right out from the heart of the perfect love. He has need of the new birth into the same Father's likeness by a Spirit That is of a better world than this, who would understand, who would do anything else than caricature, words so purposely dark as these. Nevertheless let us try to see a little way into them.

I shall suppose that my brother has done me wrong. Judgment says: Let it be so done to him. But as between him and me, two brothers, what have I to do with judgment? There is One Who judgeth. What I, his brother, owe him is not judgment, but brother's love. If love retaliate at all, it must be for public justice, never from private feeling; and with public justice, I, as an individual complainant, have no immediate concern. I ought to be willing, therefore, to bear the wrong without prejudice to my brotherliness. Yes, and then? Why, then, love on as before, so as to be no whit less ready to bear a second wrong than I was to bear that first one; or, which is better, to do him in return, not as much evil, but as much good, as he has done me evil. If my loss has been his gain (for he surely thought so at least when he wronged me), love bids me be well content that he should gain at my expense. Love bids me, if it will do him good, be content to lose as much again for him. Repay his evil with evil? I should rather repay him with good. 'Eye for eye'—his for mine? Better he should have both of mine, if they will serve his turn. It was clearly an injustice that my loss should have been his gain; for that injustice he clearly owes as much as he has unjustly taken. But private love waits not on general justice. So far from that, love takes her debtor's righteous debt of 'eye for eye' on her own head, and pays 'the just for the unjust.' 1 Pet. iii. 18. Herself she punishes, as it were; for she loses

PART I.

FOURTH ILLUSTRATION

G

what the aggressor should have lost, suffers what the evil-doer should have suffered. Once love suffered at the offender's hands, when he sinned against her; a second time she chooses to suffer in his stead, when she pays his forfeit. Is it not clear that this is just the old law of retaliation turned inside out, read after a quite new and nobler fashion? Instead of an equivalent exacted from the evil-doer, there is a redoubled kindness shown him, like coals of fire! The iron law of legal justice is transmuted by this magic of love into a golden rule of vicarious sacrifice. The sufferer is he who repays, not the aggressor. Love bears in its body the sins of its enemies; and 'God,' it is written, 'is love.'

<small>PART I.
FOURTH ILLUSTRATION

Prov. xxv. 21, 22, quoted Rom. xii. 20.

1 John iv. 8, 16.</small>

This exquisite and, as one thinks, superhuman virtue our Lord teaches, after His manner, by four concrete examples. Of course, when an instance is in this way selected to illustrate a principle, the instance is usually an extreme or next to impossible one; both because a principle is best seen when pushed to its ultimate application, and also because there is less chance of people blindly copying the example when its extravagance drives them to search for some inner meaning in it. It is conceivable that circumstances might occur in which wise love would counsel a man even to offer his other cheek to a blow, though the circumstances in which Jesus' own face was struck before the Sanhedrim did not; and sometimes it is better to suffer spoliation, as St. Paul advises, rather than go to law with a brother. But no sane man can imagine it to be kindness to give to every 'sturdy beggar' or every lazy scoundrel who wants to borrow. Our Lord, like all popular moralists, takes for granted that people bring their common sense at least to His words; and the very impossibility of keeping them to the letter is, I repeat, a hint that men should look to their hidden spirit. If ever man's words were, Jesus' are, 'spirit and life.' It needs only a little skill to see that, in all these four examples, our Lord is looking through to the feeling of love in the heart; that is, to the utter absence of all personal revenge, and the willingness, on the contrary, to suffer, not this injury only, but as much more, for the offender's good. That is the essential moral state aimed at by these injunctions. Once that is secured, it must be left to christian sagacity to discover in each case, and in view of many qualifying circumstances here left out, how the offender's good may be best attained, and the desire of a true, forgiving, and patient charity most successfully accomplished.

Marginalia: PART I. FOURTH ILLUSTRATION. 1 Cor. vi. 7. John vi. 63.

PART I.
——
FOURTH
ILLUSTRATION

Our Lord's four instances begin with the highest injuries, and descend to the lowest.

1. By general consent, a blow on the face is the extreme of personal insults; hardly ever given in ancient times but to slaves; peculiarly resented by an Oriental; only to be wiped out, according to the code of modern honour, by blood. It can hardly be doubted that our Lord's words flatly condemn the system of duelling, and those ideas of honour on which it rests. But the spirit of these words is not open to the suspicion of being a craven spirit. It is this suspicion, more, I fancy, than anything else, which is apt to discredit the teaching of this text with generous men. Yet here, as always, it is sin, not love, which is the real coward. Duelling declined from the day when men discovered that it was a practice which came easier to the bully than to the valiant gentleman. It is only needful to push this discovery to all parallel cases, to see that he who best obeys the rule of Jesus will be the bravest man. To curb temper; to govern the spirit of revenge, even under insult; to place what is better than life, personal honour, under the control of a love which is patient just because it is strong—stronger than passion: this is true valour and true honour. Jesus makes manhood

manlier by making it godlike, and teaches us a chivalry more noble than that of knighthood, by putting the cross, not on the sword-pommel, but on the heart. PART I. FOURTH ILLUSTRATION

2. Spoliation, whether under forms of law, as St. Matthew gives the next case, or by private violence, as in St. Luke's version, is a less serious wrong, because it only affects property. Our Lord urges His hearer to be prepared, before the case of extortion goes to court, to yield not merely the cheap linen under-tunic which is claimed, but over and above, if needful, the large outer plaid which is the Oriental's chief article of dress, both by night and by day. The verse is Eastern in colouring and concrete in form; but it really covers the whole principle which rules the litigation of Christians. It is under all circumstances not perhaps wrong, but at least a defect of charity, to go to law either for mere personal pique, or for the single end of private selfish gain. When this has been said, there remain plenty of considerations which in a multitude of cases will justify lawsuits. The protection of society against similar fraud, the interests or rights of one's family and dependants, the dignity of one's office, the mere assertion of right against wrong, nay, the very credit of religion, may enter so

Matt. v. 40.
Luke vi. 29.

χιτών.
ἱμάτιον.

clearly into a case as not only to justify a man in invoking the aid of public law, but even to require him to do so, as the best expression for an enlightened and upright love. Only it must be at the bidding of motives which not only justice sanctions, but love commends, if it is to be worthy of the christian citizen.

3. 'Compelling a man to go a mile' alludes to the practice of impressing runners or waggoners or guides into the transport and postal service of government. Despatch-bearers in ancient Persia, as throughout the East, were relieved, like messengers of the fiery cross in the Scottish Highlands, by committing their errand to fresh men, who were compelled to forward it to the next stage without delay. The custom gave origin to a happy proverb for any species of compulsory service; such as that of the rustic who met the procession which escorted our Lord Himself to crucifixion, and was forced to turn and bear His cross behind Him. Servants and other inferiors under harsh, troublesome, or exacting employers are perhaps the nearest parallel in modern society; and to render willingly what is ungraciously acquired is the closest fulfilment of this law which modern conditions usually admit.

4. In the case of beggars, and especially of

borrowers, the injury done descends to the lowest possible. Of course, the begging or borrowing must be both unreasonable and vexatious, otherwise there would be absolutely no injury at all; but even when it is so, there is no compulsion, except a moral one, upon the person solicited. In this case, it is not refusal to give or to lend which is prohibited; for refusal may be, and very often is, a duty. It is such refusal as proceeds from unwillingness to oblige, or is caused or aggravated by impatience and irritation. Such refusal is wrong, because it indicates a want of endurance or of self-denial in one's love; and plainly, giving may be so done as to argue exactly the same want. To give, as the unjust judge did, merely because the petitioner's pertinacity teases you, or because his presence offends you, not only may be no charity, but may actually argue as great a lack of charity as refusing would. There are few departments of social duty in which it is harder for us to be wisely kind than in this. On the one hand, beggars may be worthless and borrowers cheats, so that it is difficult to give and not do harm by giving: yet even in the worst of our cities there are deserving poor; and we have all need to hear the old words of the son of Sirach: 'Refuse not the prayer of the wretched, and turn

PART I.

FOURTH ILLUSTRATION

Luke xviii. 2-5.

Ecclus. iv. 4-6.

not thine eyes from the needy, lest he complain against thee; for He Who has made him heareth his petition, when with sorrowful heart he complaineth against thee.' On the other hand, it is as hard to withhold alms with the firm and unprovoked temper of true kindness, when beggars are teasing and borrowers shameless: yet even the rude, the whining, the dishonest, and the thankless, are our brothers; and if we owe it to them not to encourage vice by heedless liberality, we also owe it to them not to let our refusals be dictated by annoyance or embittered by surliness. It ought to be easier than it is for comfortable people to bear with the starving and friendless poor, even when their mendicant cry is an unseasonable interruption to business or sport; even though they are a little too eager to tell, and too slow to cease, the voluble story of their distress. It is often our duty to refuse; but it is a duty of which love should take all the pain, making it to them as painless as possible in the doing of it.

Thus, with intimate knowledge of our common life, does Jesus trace the workings of revengeful irritation down from the buffet which burns upon the cheek, to the neighbour who only pesters us with his borrowing. Everywhere He bids us substitute for the passion which calls for retaliation, that nobler charity which repays evil with good. Shallow or selfish hearts are apt to say this is to put a premium on aggression, and meekly invite a repetition of it. No doubt there are foolish ways of yielding a literal obedience to this law, which would have no better effect than to provoke a second blow on the other cheek. Yet love is wise, not foolish; and often wiser in its generous confidence than selfishness in its calculating suspiciousness, which it terms prudence. God has made human souls more susceptible, on the whole, to kindness than to any other moral force; and such kindness as this, which can not only forgive, but suffer, offence, is fit to melt the rock and to tame the brute. Good, by the simple and lovely strength of its own goodness, does in the end overcome evil; or if it does not, it is because evil cannot be overcome. At all events, when a patient lover of men is trying, by unaffected meekness and unrequited generosity, to wear out the evil-doing of the bad and shame them into penitence, he is only taking the course which both God's wisdom has prescribed and God's own love has followed. It is not by His words only, but much more by His acts, that Jesus has fulfilled this law which substitutes

PART I.

FOURTH
ILLUSTRATION

PART I.
FOURTH
ILLUSTRATION

generosity for revenge. In His person we see the supreme example of His own rule. We see, in fact, the Divinity descending to repay the injuries of His creatures, not with just vengeance, but with the self-sacrifice of love; taking not only our buffet, but the penalty for the buffet too; and trusting to draw all hearts unto Himself through no charm but the charm of love lifted up for us on its self-chosen painful cross.

O suffering Son of God! Best Interpreter of Thine own law! We have made Thee to serve with our sins; yet Thou hast taken the form of a servant, and ministered to our necessities. We sought to rob Thee of Thine honour; but Thou didst make Thyself poorer still for us, and of no reputation. We smote Thee on the right cheek by our sins; and Thou hast turned the other also to the chastisement of our peace. Daily we come to importune Thee by endless petitions and calls for mercy; but to every one who asks Thou givest liberally without upbraiding, and from the guiltiest Thou turnest not away. So hast Thou heaped upon all our heads Thy coals of fire!

Teach us, dear Lord, the might of Thy love,

and persuade our cold, unloving hearts to dare to copy Thee in Thy magnanimity and in the ventures of Thy generosity: being to each other as meek and patient and unwearied in service as Thou hast been to all of us; for Thy Name's glory, and Thy Kingdom's sake. Amen.

FIFTH ILLUSTRATION:

WHO IS MY NEIGHBOUR?

Ye have heard that it hath been said, ' Thou shalt love thy neighbour, and hate thine enemy :' but I say unto you, Love your enemies, bless them that curse you, do good to them that hate you, and pray for them which despitefully use you, and persecute you; that ye may be the children of your Father Which is in heaven: for He maketh His sun to rise on the evil and on the good, and sendeth rain on the just and on the unjust. For if ye love them which love you, what reward have ye? do not even the publicans the same? And if ye salute your brethren only, what do ye more than others? do not even the publicans so? Be ye therefore perfect, even as your Father Which is in heaven is perfect.—MATT. V. 43–48.

But I say unto you which hear, Love your enemies, do good to them which hate you, bless them that curse you, and pray for them which despitefully use you. . . . For if ye love them which love you, what thank have ye? for sinners also love those that love them. And if ye do good to them which do good to you, what thank have ye? for sinners also do even the same. And if ye lend to them of whom ye hope to receive, what thank have ye? for sinners also lend to sinners, to receive as much again. But love ye your enemies, and do good, and lend, hoping for nothing again; and your reward shall be great, and ye shall be the children of the Highest: for He is kind unto the unthankful and to the evil. Be ye therefore merciful, as your Father also is merciful.—LUKE VI. 27, 28, 32–36.

WHO IS MY NEIGHBOUR?

THESE verses form our Lord's fifth and closing example of His general principle, that His relation to previous laws was one of fulfilment, not of destruction. Substantially, they deal with the same subject as the verses last considered. It is still the law of love which Jesus vindicates in its breadth against pharisaic limitations. It is still the duty of returning good for evil which He urges against the selfishness of mankind. But the limitation against which He now protests is not the same as the limitation against which He has just been protesting. Last time, the mistake lay in this, that private love was limited as to its action by a principle of criminal law. This time the mistake is, that private love was limited as to its objects through a policy of national separatism. In the former case, the question was: When does my neighbour deserve to be treated with severity, not kindness? Here the question is: Who is my neigbbour? This will appear if

PART I.

FIFTH ILLUSTRATION

we examine the popular rule quoted and criticised by our Lord.

When the Hebrew doctors said, 'Thou shalt love thy neighbour, and hate thine enemy,' they took the first half of this rule from a golden sentence in Leviticus : 'Thou shalt love thy neighbour as thyself.' The New Testament makes a great deal of that summary of duty. No fewer than three several times do we find our Lord appeal to it as embracing the pith of the whole second table of the decalogue ; and after His example it is twice cited in the letters of St. Paul, and once by St. James. Of course, thoughtful students of the Hebrew canon must always have felt it to be one of its profoundest ethical axioms. But the current teaching of our Lord's day broke down the force of the glorious old saying, not only or so much by forgetting the important words 'as thyself,' which made man's selfishness the very measure of his charity, as by narrowing that area of neighbourliness within which charity is commanded. The question of casuistry by which entangled consciences sought to evade a duty far too wide for them, was the question a lawyer put once to Jesus : 'Who is my neighbour ? ' There was a great deal in the historical attitude of the Hebrew people to suggest such a question. Every small, vigorous, and united people within which the sense of clanship is strong, and whose struggle for independent national life has forced it to look on surrounding nations as hostile, is tempted to read the law of kindness as binding only between fellow-countrymen. With the Hebrew, this temptation was stronger than in the case of any other race. Israel was always a people apart. The condition of its national existence was isolation. So much was this the case, that in the original statute 'thy neighbour' meant simply 'thy brother Jew.' Not because it excluded Gentiles of purpose, but just because, being given to Jews as a Jewish code, it took no notice whatever of foreigners. A special clause, indeed, was added, bringing within the scope of this law of love every stranger who dwelt with them in the land as a proselyte from heathenism to Judaism. But as to their private relations with foreigners who were not proselytes but heathens, the law gave no such instructions, simply because it forbade them to have relations with heathen foreigners at all. It contemplated, as the normal condition of Israel, an entire seclusion of the Jew from any private social intercourse with the uncircumcised. The individual Jew was to have no 'neighbours' save

PART I.

FIFTH ILLUSTRATION

Lev. xix. 34.

H

Jews. Even the commonwealth was, as far as possible, to preserve in its external politics the same separatist attitude. Its relations with neighbouring states were to be, as nearly as practicable, no relations at all. Intercourse with conterminous heathendom was sure to mean in any case temptation, and most probably corruption. Peace there might be with idolatrous states—with Egypt, with Phœnicia, with Assyria; but it was to be the peace of indifference, not of alliance. Throughout the whole of Jewish history, any drawing close of the bonds of political friendship between the chosen people and adjacent heathen empires was looked on by pious Jews as a perilous and un-Jewish policy, false to the divine vocation of the race. Nay, in so far as any other policy than one of isolation was enjoined, it was a policy of hostility. Close in on the flanks of Hebrew territory lay several border tribes somewhat allied to Israel in blood. Contact with these was inevitable; but with them the danger of interfusion was greatest, and the terms to be held with them were explicitly prescribed. None of the race of Ammon or of Moab could become a Jewish proselyte; and while a milder tone was used of the more cognate Edomites, the tribe of Amalek was devoted to such annihilation,

Marginal notes: PART I. FIFTH ILLUSTRATION. Cf. e.g. Isa. viii. 5-14; Hos. vii. 8-16. Deut. xxiii. 3-6. Ibid. ver. 7. Deut. xxv. 17-19.

that its very memory was to perish. Within Hebrew territory itself there lingered remnants of the powerful aboriginal races which it had been Israel's mission to dispossess. With them they were to be on still worse terms. No friendly league was ever to be contracted. On the contrary, Israel was bound over by its earliest constitution to pursue the Canaanitish tribes with relentless and unquenchable hostility. Whatever public reasons of weight there were to justify this rule of national politics, it never could be meant for a moment to dictate the feeling of individuals or prescribe how in private life a Jew was to treat a Philistine. At the same time, it was perfectly natural that this isolation from other races imposed on the Hebrews, their jealous fear of defilement from foreign contact, the religious conceit bred by such separatism, and the national feud kept up with their next neighbours from generation to generation, should all have formed a fitting soil for the growth of bigotry, pride of race, superciliousness, and hereditary hatred. It is extremely intelligible how the ordinary Jew should never have passed beyond the earliest and narrowest sense of the word 'neighbour,' but have continued to restrict his whole sympathy and human interest to people of his own land, religion,

PART I.

FIFTH ILLUSTRATION

Ex. xxiii. 32, 33; Num. xxxiii. 50–56; Deut. vii. 1–6, xx. 15–18 (cf. Josh. x. 28–41).

and blood. It is to the glory of the Jewish race, indeed, that there were men at many a moment in its history who could separate between the hostility which they owed to idolaters as public enemies of the theocracy, and the humanity which they owed to them as men. Statesmen and seers whose moral stature rose as high as that of Moses, or David, or Daniel, or Nehemiah, might never suffer their patriotic and religious zeal to degenerate into personal hate; but this could not be looked for from common natures. The average Jew of Saul's day smote Amalek with the ferocity of individual passion, just as the average Jew of Christ's day spurned the fellowship of the Greek with a bitter personal scorn. It is the inevitable consequence of all separatism, prerogative, and monopoly; of every advantage which sets man above man, race above race, and which either may not or cannot be made the equal property of all,—that from such a root springs the bitter fruit of uncharitableness. This, however, was not all. Having gone this length in circumscribing humanity, the next step was an easy one. Once the Jew read his law in this sense: 'Thou shalt love thy neighbour Jew, and hate thy Gentile enemy,' it was natural to go a little further, and exclude from love's pale even

Jews who became as Gentiles through their enmity. If every foreigner and heathen is my enemy, as well as an enemy to the state, and therefore to be hated, not loved; why may not my fellow-clansman become more of an enemy to me, do me more hurt, and deserve more hate, than any far-off Gentile of them all? It is simply as an enemy of mine that any man—Jew, why not, as well as heathen?—deserves no love. Such a man is no more my 'neighbour.' He is to me as a heathen man. He is to be hated. So reasoned in these Jews the cruel human heart that is in all of us. So it thrust its petty selfishness into the very large and loving law of God. Words which He meant to be wide enough to hold humanity, are contracted to just as narrow a circle of near friends or comrades as any man chooses; and the divine law is travestied by a word so inhuman, so devilish, as this: 'Thou shalt love thy neighbour, and hate thine enemy.'

The immediate protest of Jesus against this rider to the words of the law taught nothing which was absolutely new. It is rather common to hear love for enemies spoken of as a precept peculiar to the New Testament—a glory of Christian morals with no parallel elsewhere. The truth

PART I.
——
FIFTH
ILLUSTRATION
Ex. xxiii. 4, 5.

is, that even in the book of Exodus the law of Moses commanded every Hebrew to help his enemy in his straits: 'If thou meet thine enemy's ox or his ass going astray, thou shalt surely bring it back to him again. If thou see the ass of him that hateth thee lying under his burden, and wouldest forbear to help him, thou shalt surely help him.' The kindly spirit which dictated these small injunctions to every-day acts of neighbourliness is precisely the spirit of the great Teacher on the mount; and by a tribe of simple Orientals, such small precepts would be better understood than any wider principle of ethics. In a more literary age of Hebrew history, the same spirit reappears in an admonition against even secret exultation over an adversary's mishaps. 'Rejoice not,' said the Preacher, 'when thine enemy falleth, and let not thine heart be glad when he stumbleth; lest the Lord see it, and it displease Him.' This is very noble teaching, and Hebrew annals can show as noble examples. The brotherly forgiveness of Joseph, the meekness of Moses, and the magnanimity of David, who was, if any man was, the typical hero of the Hebrews: these gave to their countrymen examples of generosity in the treatment of private enemies brilliant enough to be worth a

Prov. xxiv. 17, 18; cf. the protest of Job, xxxi. 29, 30.

thousand moral maxims. When Jesus, therefore, reiterated His vigorous commands: 'Love your enemies, bless them that curse you, do good to them that hate you,' and so on, He only put into sharper and more memorable words a law which had been from the beginning. Moses would have recognised in these words his own rule, David his own practice; and heathendom itself has had its teachers who in substance taught: 'Thou shalt love thy neighbour, even though he be thine enemy.'

What was more characteristic in the teaching of Jesus as a Hebrew moralist, was the breaking down of that national particularism which, from the formation of the commonwealth, had made every Jew, indeed, the Jew's neighbour, but every foreigner his foe. It was not in the Sermon on the Mount, it was in the weighty parable of the good Samaritan, spoken later, that He expressly unbound the term 'neighbour,' and levelled the walls of religious bigotry, of race jealousy, and of national seclusion, in order to set man in brotherhood with man all the world over. I am not sure that this clear and firm assertion of the universal brotherhood of men, implying as it does their essential spiritual equality, is not one of the most signal services which His

Part I.

Fifth Illustration

Luke x. 30 ff.

teaching rendered to the moral thought of the world. Whatever vagaries—stupid or frantic vagaries—men may play with these catchwords, 'fraternity,' and 'equality;' however such terms may become the *Shibboleths* of political fanaticism, or carry to the frightened ears of society recollections of carnage, rapine, and conflagration : their origin at least is divine. They are of christian descent; they carry by right a blessed and beneficent signification. That every man is every other man's equal in God's sight, has already abolished many a gross shape of bondage; it will yet abolish shapes less gross. That human brotherhood is as wide as humanity, has already brought the ends of the earth into a more cosmopolitan relationship; it will yet federate the nations into a compacter unity. That each man owes loving help to every other man who needs it and to him most who is nearest to him, has already created christian philanthropy; and it may yet teach us how to bind social classes in gentler and more elastic bonds of mutual support than political economy has been able to weave. Christianity is not responsible for all the folly and blundering which, like froth from ferment, has been bred by christian ideas in human brains. But for *this* it is responsible : for the teaching which suffers no private man, on any plea of personal or public enmity, or of class estrangement, or of alien blood, or of hostile faiths, or of simple selfish indifference and luxurious ease, to stand still and see another man suffer without relief, or perish without an effort to save ; for this it is responsible, because this is the teaching of Jesus Christ.

I have said that it is in the story of the good Samaritan that this part of Christ's teaching comes out most fully; but I find its ground and germ in what is here said about the fatherly love of God. For what does He say?—'Love your enemies, and do them good, as well as your friends, in order that your love may be like God's. God is your Father in heaven. It is the son's mark and glory to be like his father. Now the chief characteristic of the divine goodness is, that it is over all, wide as His works, embracing evil as well as good. So wide, so unconfined, so free from selfishness and passion, ought your love to be, if you would carry on your soul the family features of the sons of God.' In this teaching lies the germ of all christian teaching on the subject. Is God our Father in heaven?—then are we all brethren. Does He show love to all men with paternal impartiality?—then are we all in His sight essentially equal. Those barriers which are raised by ancestry, climate, education, or society, to sunder brother-men, and make them no true neighbours to each other, oppose no obstacle to His equal bounty, Who is the Maker and the Parent of us all; neither ought they any longer to limit our good offices. Here, in Jesus, mankind has found its common Father; mankind becomes, in consequence, one family of brothers.

To drive His lesson home, Jesus reaches round for some simple popular example of God's impartial goodness: He finds it in sun and rain. Sun and rain are neither the most precious nor the most astonishing proofs of the kindness of the Father for His evil no less than for His good children. The Speaker Himself, sent of the Father to bear our sins, to lighten our darkness, and to revive our death; Christ, sending abroad to all men everywhere the same glad words of reconciliation, like far-shooting shafts of spiritual light, and pouring out on all men His quickening Spirit, like showers that water the earth—He was and is the grandest instance of God's impartial 'philanthropy,' and the love which blesses the evil and the good. But the time was not then come when this instance could be published, nor were His audience prepared to hear it. Jesus reads a lesson from an humbler book, which lies for ever

open before all men's eyes. Let those who tread
God's earth and look up into His sky day after
day, without a thought of what these so silently
are preaching, hearken to this Interpréter of
nature. Many a year through had He hearkened
to the 'still small voice' of earth and sky, as He
walked about the white slopes of upland Nazareth;
and now He tells us what message had been
borne to Him from His Father on every sun-
beam—what words came dancing to the earth
in every raindrop. Has God left His children
without a witness to His love? Was no message
sent to the great old world before Christ came?
none to the uncounted heathens of to-day? none
to the emigrant, the seaman, the souls who hear
no Sabbath bell and have no written Word to
read? Nay, verily; but 'in that He did good, Acts xiv. 17.
and gave us rain from heaven and fruitful seasons,
filling our hearts with food and gladness,' God
hath not 'left Himself without witness.' The
sweet and bounteous influences of the seasons,
in their ceaseless and impartial bestowal, have
always told in a speech which, without a voice, Ps. xix. 1-4.
goes to the end of the world, how the heavenly
Father loveth even the world of men who hate
Him, and hath blessings for such as curse Him.
Take your stand on some glorious day in June

[margin: PART I. — FIFTH ILLUSTRATION]

PART I.

FIFTH ILLUSTRATION

on a rising ground, with a fair broad English landscape spread around you, bathed in warm sunlight. Overhead the unconfined and generous sky bends, large and full-armed, as if to brood in nursing love over the growing earth—oldest and best emblem of the all-nurturing Father. Away on every side, to farthest line of vision, rolls wave on wave of ridge and hollow, field and copse, upland and meadow. Men have parcelled it out, not without old bickerings and bloodshed long forgotten, and the ancient landmarks they guard with jealousy. But the sunlight heeds no fence. With impartial warmth, it lies on either side the hedge which parts the lands of rival squires, nor cares for the ancestral feud which has made them foes. It falls on the hind at work, and his heart is lightened. It falls through the cottage pane on the sick girl's coverlet; and as she turns twenty times in an hour to the glad light, she calls herself better than she felt last night. It falls on the children at play on the village-green, and they shout the louder for it in their mirth. It falls on the song-bird on the bough, and he whistles out his soul for joy. Has it no message, that glory, like the smile of God, which 'looketh upon all things' to bless them?

Ecclus. xlii. 16.

Wait, then, till the heavy rain-cloud comes trailing across country before the south-west breeze, and you shall see how impartially it too will fall. Yonder lie two fields, with but a thread of darker green to part them. That to the right has a churl and a cheat for its owner, a man who underpays his hinds, grudges the poor their alms, can rob the widow and cajole the orphan, a man whose little godless soul worships the clay he owns, yet stints the very soil its just and needful nourishment. The neighbouring field is tilled with patient and generous care by an honest man, whose name the cottagers name with a blessing. See now, how the swift shadow of God's cloud sweeps nearer, and the big drops begin to fall! Would you have it bend from its straight course to fertilize the furrows of the righteous man, and leave the other's unwatered? He Who steers its way as His breath propels it, is the Father of both, and His impartial love pours as lavish treasure on the enemy as on the friend. What does this impartiality of nature tell us? What glad tidings of its Almighty Maker does it bring to His human children? That everything is moved by blind machinery, and has behind its iron laws no feeling personal heart at all?—that either there is no God, or at least no revelation of His character in the rigid system of physical

PART I.

FIFTH ILLUSTRATION

forces which we call nature? The dreary creed of scientific materialism, into which so many seek just now to shut us up, is as much against those filial instincts of our human heart, which cry aloud after a God Who is our Father, as they are against Him Who was manifest in history to show us the Father, that our hearts might be satisfied. Or shall we say that God, Whose sun shines so equally on all, cares nothing for either good or bad, and hath neither love nor hate? That were no gospel for any man to hear, nor a lesson any man could believe. No; but impartial nature has this good news to tell, that the Father in heaven cares for all His children, and is patient with the evil among them, and is not willing to punish, but waits to pardon. To the good He is good, delighting to bless; to the evil also He is not evil, but meanwhile good, being slow to anger. By forbearance, by showing the loving-kindness of His heart, by doing good unweariedly 'to the unthankful and the evil,' the Father strives to win back His children; in them He seeks to provoke some faint shame, some feeble desire after their Father and His favour. As the 'beloved brother Paul' has written to us, this common goodness of God to unjust and evil men is meant to lead them to repentance, and is therefore a testimony wide as the earth to the largeness of the Father's love; a very gospel of mercy and hope to the whole race; a sermon in every tongue on this text, that God is One Who will bless them that curse Him, and do good to those who hate Him.

The words of this gospel according to nature shine in new clearness and speak more intelligibly, now that we have also the better gospel according to Jesus Christ. Another Sun is risen on our spiritual night, and it is on the evil His rays fall. 'God commendeth His love toward us, in that, while we were yet sinners, Christ died for us. . . . When we were enemies, we were reconciled to God by the death of His Son.' The messenger who flies abroad in the midst of our sky, shedding spiritual light on every man, tells, but tells more mightily, the same lesson as the sunshine. He proclaims the Father's catholic charity, His unrestricted love for His fallen and evil children, and bids all men everywhere alike have hope, and arise, and return. Another rain, too, has begun to drop from the Father's heaven. It droppeth on the just, but also on the unjust. 'If ye, being evil, know how to give good gifts unto your children, how much more shall your heavenly Father give the Holy Spirit to them that ask Him!' Rain of gracious influence on arid and sterile

PART I.

FIFTH ILLUSTRATION

Rom. v. 8, 10.

Cf. Rev. xiv. 6, c. John i. 9.

Luke xi. 13; cf. Matt. vii. 11.

PART I.

FIFTH ILLUSTRATION

John xiii. 34;
cf. Eph. v. 2
and 1 John
iii. 16.

hearts; rain to revive the weary and fructify the fruitless; rain to be had for the asking, impartial and free! Behold the nature-lesson of Jesus re-read in His own history: on the cross and at Pentecost the old, old message that God loves all, even His enemies, became a new message, laden with new gladness and charged with a new power. The children of God are bound to love one another, as He has loved them. For them it is not enough to love as the world loves—lovers, family, and friends. Beautiful as such love is, which our Father puts into evil hearts, it is not to be the limit, though it is the centre, of christian affection. The love which comes of instinct and is measured by nearness of neighbourhood, is good. The love which has a moral root, acts on principle, and keeps no measure, but, like God, can love the worst and deny itself for the meanest; that is better, is best of all. Up to this godlike attitude of self-denying and generous charity our Lord calls His followers. To follow Him thither; to copy His style of loving; to stoop, to bear, to forgive, to seek, to save, to overflow and reach out, to embrace all men in our hearts, and spend for them our lives; this is, saith Jesus, christian perfection. It is to be not less noble, less generous, or less munificent than the Father of all. This is a giddy height. Can human feet stand as high? Up Jesus will lead us by easiest steps: by lessons of sunshine and cloud; by doing of plain and simple works; by saluting men who are not our brethren; by cultivating a larger courtesy and a less partial kindness in daily intercourse; by learning to pray for our persecutors; by calling every man a neighbour, and being his good Samaritan: thus, along a not too steep yet arduous enough path of moral tuition, will He guide us, if we will try to follow, till even our feet also stand upon the dazzling pavement of celestial virtue, and we too are become 'perfect, even as our Father Which is in heaven is perfect.'

PART II.

THE LAW OF SECRECY IN RELIGION.

THE PRINCIPLE:

BEFORE GOD, NOT MEN.

Take heed that ye do not your alms ['righteousness'] before men, to be seen of them: otherwise ye have no reward of your Father Which is in heaven.—MATT. VI. 1.

THE PRINCIPLE: BEFORE GOD, NOT MEN.

THE first eighteen verses of the sixth chapter form one connected paragraph of our Lord's discourse, which in its substance complements the last paragraph, and in its structure resembles it.

PART II.

THE PRINCIPLE.

In the last paragraph, Jesus laid down His central principle at the outset: that His relation to the earlier or Mosaic legislation was not destruction, but fulfilment; and this principle He illustrated by a series of five examples. The exactly parallel structure of this next paragraph is perhaps concealed from the reader by an error in the received text. If, with the oldest MSS. and the best critics, we read for 'alms' in the opening verse the more general word 'righteousness,'[1] new light will be cast on the whole pas-

Matt. v. 17-48.

Ver. 17.

vi. 1-18.

---

[1] So Tischendorf, Meyer, Tholuck, and others read, with B, D, Vat., Sin., etc. It is possible, however, that since צדקה (= righteousness) is the standing Old Testament term for alms, and in that sense is sometimes rendered by the LXX. ἰλεημοσύνη, the variation of reading in this verse may not indicate any real variation in the sense. May not both Greek words represent the same Aramaic word, either in the mind of the evangelist or in the usage of our Lord Himself?

sage. For then we have first of all the general principle laid down as before—the principle that righteousness is not to be done for the purpose of display; and on this there follows, as before, a series of examples. The three subdivisions of what the later Jews termed 'righteousness,' using that word technically in the sense of religious service, were almsgiving, prayers, and fasting; and to each of these in succession our Lord applies His central principle.

As these two large sections of the Sermon thus correspond in their structure, so they have also a deeper relation to one another. The word 'righteousness' in the opening verses of this section may not exactly answer to the same word 'righteousness' as used in the opening verses of the last section; because it appears to be borrowed from the phraseology of the Pharisees and to bear a conventional and narrower signification: it is the 'righteousness' which made up in their estimation a devout or religious character. But at least this choice of the same word to start with afresh must be meant to look back upon the starting-point of the discussion just closed; and we are driven to search for some inner connection between the thoughts.[1] We find it, I think,

---

[1] If the reading δὲ (after προσέχετε), which Tischendorf and

in this, that what the preceding section did for the rule of righteousness, this section does for its motive. What Jesus has been doing is to correct the literal interpretation of the law of righteousness, which is also its narrow interpretation, by reading the law in its spirit, and showing that, so read, it is very broad. In one example after another, He has read beneath the letter of each commandment its informing spirit of love; and as, time after time, He used this spirit of love as a canon of interpretation, the law has become in His hands, instead of easier, harder to be kept. For, in pointing to the spirit of each action as the true seat of its goodness or badness, rightness or wrongness, He has widened the area of law, till it covers, not behaviour only, but intention; thought as well as deed; the inward even more than the outward life of men. We are thus led to feel that, even when we do what is undeniably a good or righteous action, it is not the action alone we have to look to, but the motive from which it proceeds. From the sphere of law, so understood, we naturally pass to the motive of obedience. Now, among human actions there were three sorts, which the somewhat ascetic

PART II.

THE PRINCIPLE.

Meyer adopt, and which has the authority of the Sinaitic, be correct, such a connection will have a textual ground.

PART II.
THE PRINCIPLE.

and very artificial piety of the time insisted on as acts of eminent goodness. Other things might be right to do; but to give alms, say prayers, and keep fasts, composed the 'righteousness' of saintly or exceptionally good people. It was, indeed, a miserable narrowing of human righteousness, that righteousness whose ideal was not short of the perfection of God, to shut it up within three such formal exercises of religious worship; but this mistake, which later Judaism shared with all systems in which the religious element has outgrown the moral, Jesus had already sufficiently exposed. Another evil remained. When righteousness is shrivelled down to a set of religious usages, these usages themselves tend to become sapless and unreal. The same evaporation of the spirit of love, and the same preference for the letter over the inner meaning of the law, which led men to call alms, prayers, and fasts their 'righteousness,' led them also to fast, pray, and give alms for the praise of men rather than from the love of God. Current Jewish limitations of the sphere of righteousness Jesus had corrected by the former principle of spirituality in the law's interpretation; the current perversion of motive in such righteousness as they did recognise He now corrects by the principle of secrecy in religion.

It is not the visibility of one's sacred duties to which Jesus takes objection; for in an earlier part of this Sermon He has already taught that the good deeds of His disciples must be not only visible, but luminous; nor luminous only, but conspicuous. It is the purpose to attract attention which is condemned. That vitiates the act by substituting a selfish for a noble motive. That is to put man in God's place of judgment. That therefore robs the doer of all merit in the eye of God. To do your righteous acts, says Jesus, in the presence of men, in order to be looked at by them as a spectacle,[1] is to forfeit the reward of the heavenly Father. Few words in Holy Writ are more fundamental or searching than this; for there lies at the root of such a principle this still deeper truth, that the merit of a good action consists not in its motive merely, but in the godliness of its motive. Righteousness is not just an affair betwixt man and man, as it appears to be in the half-pagan philosophy of our ethical schools. Even the schools, indeed, demand that some nobler and less interested motive than the love of applause should inspire men with virtue. But the ethic of Jesus goes further. For an

PART II.

THE PRINCIPLE.
See Matt. v. 14–16.

---

[1] θιαθῆναι implies being looked at '*cum studio et admiratione.*' See Tittmann, *de Synonymis N. T.* pp. 120, 121.

audience of admiring bystanders, He is not content to substitute — as our systems do — the approval of the good man's own conscience, or an abstract love of virtue for its own sake, or an enlightened regard to the welfare of the greatest number: what He does substitute is God. God is the sole audience and the sole spectator of the Christian. Himself unseen, He sees the hidden process of emotion and purpose which precedes action, as well as the act itself; and as He was our Lawgiver at the first, Whose will each actor is bound to consult, so shall He be our Judge at last, by Whose sentence actions must be weighed. According to christian teaching, therefore, religion is the soul of morals. The conscience of each man is withdrawn from the crowd of onlookers who observe and criticise his outward conduct. He is set free from their censure and the craving to please them. He is placed in immediate and confidential relations with the supreme Onlooker, Who is too remote to be touched by earthly misconceptions, for He is in heaven; yet not so remote as to be out of sympathy, for He is our Father. The rule of duty ceases to be an uninformed voice of our own nature, or a code generalized from the experience of mankind, or the average moral sentiment of a community. It becomes the revealed law of the divine commandments. Righteousness comes to mean just obedience; such obedience as a child will pay to the expressed will of a perfect Parent. Merit,[1] in the divine eyes, will be in proportion to the singleness, purity, and unselfishness of the man's desire to serve and please his heavenly Father. And morality, 'righteousness,' whether in its narrower or wider sense, becomes a sacred, secret, devout thing, hid away in that holy of holies of the religious nature in which worship dwells. Is it needful to point out how entirely this carrying of ethics up into godliness cuts away by the roots that sham holiness of one-sided religionists of which we have the type in Pharisaism? It not less cuts down on the other side the shallow utilitarian morality of our own day, which thinks it can do without any basis outside of humanity—the righteousness which has parted company with godliness. Unnatural in Christ's eyes must be any severance of these two; for to Him these two have one life: godliness is the root of righteousness, and righteousness the fruit of godliness.

The bearing of all this on our Lord's warning in the text is not far to seek. Since that only

---

[1] Merit, that is, not in the sense of claim on the reward, but of moral fitness to receive it.

PART II.
THE
PRINCIPLE.

which is done out of a regard to God's approval is well done, it follows that, in strict fact, the Christian in his actions knows nothing of any other witness. To him, so far as any practical influence on his moral state is concerned, privacy and publicity are words without meaning. He acts the same before men as alone; for he is never 'alone' from that one Spectator Whom he seeks to please, and Who sees in secret; nor can the company of a crowd increase or lessen his desire to please that one Spectator. One Presence fills, possesses, dominates the man whose passion it is to be righteous before the face of his Father in heaven. But let him once become so conscious of the observation of others, that with his desire to please the judging Father and win His reward, there shall mingle some desire to please also his human witnesses, and win their admiration; instantly his singleness of aim grows confused, the purity of his motive is clouded, and the divine acceptableness of his service suffers. The entrance of this dual reference is full of peril. The man has need, in Jesus' words, to 'take heed.' Nothing is so easy as to let a regard to the notice and approbation of our fellows edge out of its place first our exclusive, and by and by our supreme, regard to the judgment of the Father. Our fellow-men are beside us; we see that they observe us; the signs of their admiration or censure are present, and not to be mistaken. Whereas He Who sees in secret dwells also in a secret place; that He sees us at all, or cares to note what we do, is a thing to be taken on trust; if He is passing on us any present judgment, at least it may be long before we know it, or reap either reward from His approval or pain from His displeasure. Here, as always, it is the present which thrusts aside the future; the seen, the unseen; and sense, faith.

PART II.

THE PRINCIPLE.

Cf. 2 Cor. iv. 18.

It does not at all follow that a man's outward behaviour will change when this change of motive occurs. Man may have displaced God as witness, umpire, and rewarder of righteousness; and yet the same righteous acts may continue to be done, and done as diligently or punctiliously as before. The man is fallen from a son of God into a slave of human criticism; but no eye which does not see in secret can at first detect the fall. His righteousness has ceased to receive reward from God; but it is not given to us to discern the spiritual worth of human conduct, and the subtle change passes unobserved. Nevertheless, this corruption of the motive works disastrously on practical conduct. For when a man's design in behaving well is to be looked at, then the presence of human witnesses becomes essential. To be in society means then to be on one's good behaviour. To be alone, where only God sees,—the one Witness Whose inspection I have ceased to fear, the one Judge Whose approbation I do not crave,—this is to be without the motive which moved me to be righteous. Whatever restraint the presence of human spectators may impose on passion, is lifted when the man escapes from observation; and just because his virtue was a thing of restraint and not of choice, does he make up by the licence he privately allows himself for the violence he has done himself in public. Thus the life splits itself more and more into two halves: the righteous life played before men, and the self-indulgent life lived in secret. An appearance of devotion, or propriety, or benevolence, is sustained where the conduct is seen; because it is only where it is seen that any sufficient motive exists for being generous, or decorous, or devout. But it is to external conduct only that this consideration applies. The inner life, lived even in their presence, is not visible to those who have been installed the censors or rewarders of righteousness; and therefore it is but the appearance of goodness, and nothing more, which it is either needful or even possible to sustain. What passes now for such a man's righteousness is but a stage performance, at which his neighbours assist as at a spectacle. He has fabricated for himself a double life, of which the visible half is fair but false, and the secret half real but foul. The man is literally what his name of 'hypocrite' signifies, a play-actor. He only personates righteousness for applause; he walks the earth an incarnate falsehood.

'Take heed' is the warning addressed to His first Twelve, in their first days of fresh sincerity; a warning sharpened by the sight of full-blown hypocrites filling at that moment the high places of their fatherland, and the 'seats' where prophets once and just men had sat. Of this spiritual plague the beginnings are as slight as the issues are fatal. Besides, the temptation to act from a regard to public opinion rather than from the fear of God is one which, singularly enough, lies specially near to men with a reputation for religion. The fact is certain, whether the reasons be apparent or not. One reason may be, that as a reputation for piety is hard to win, so it is easy to lose. The world expects a great deal from persons who imply a rebuke on itself by professing exceptional godliness; and it

PART II.
THE PRINCIPLE.

visits any decline from that standard with corresponding severity. It judges more severely the inconsistencies of religious men than the flat immoralities of others. Hence there is the strongest reason why he who has once enjoyed a character for religion should strive to keep, and dread to lose, it. No doubt he will keep it best by thinking least about it. A single eye to his true Master will be the surest way of walking straight; and to care little about men's censure is in the majority of cases to ensure at least their respect, if not their praise. Still, these are hard things to practise; and when a good man finds that his character for goodness is both very fragrant and very easily blown upon, he is apt to watch over it with an unhealthy jealousy, to ask what men will say when he ought to be asking what God wills, and to eke out the goodness he really possesses by just the least bit of occasional assumption, in talk or manner, of more goodness still. Add to this, that those parts of righteousness which belong most to its religious side are those which lend themselves most readily to imitation, and it will be seen why hypocrisy should be characteristically the religionist's vice. To persuade society that you are honest while you are cheating it, or chaste when you are licentious, is rather hard. Plain round duties of every-day morality are easily tested; and comparatively few will try to wear a mask which is so sure to be torn off. But the higher and more inward side of virtue, its Godward aspect, is absolutely screened from the direct inspection of society; and if it betray itself at all, must betray itself by certain outward signs or acts which are very imitable. The three stock exercises of good Pharisees, for example, of which Jesus goes on to speak, are pretty much the characteristic outcome of piety in every age of the world. With regard to every one of these, it is exceedingly easy to perform the visible act, and exceedingly difficult to tell what feeling is hidden under it. Anybody who has money to spare can give alms, and pass for charitable; prayers are as easily said by a knave as by a saint; while he who cares to fast, may fast, whatever his reason for it be. The actions of piety, like its tones or its gaits, are so imitable, and the imitation is so hard of detection, that they become the invariable livery of the hypocrite. For the very same reason, they seduce those who are not as yet hypocrites into becoming so. When a man would increase or preserve a reputation for piety which he has once honestly enough obtained, it is fatally easy to perform pious acts, with this end in view, a little oftener or a little more ostentatiously than he would do were he careful only about serving God. Thus one gets, commonly before one quite knows it, on that inclined plane of men-pleasing and false appearances, the end of which is death. 'Take heed,' said Jesus.

No one who has so much as read the Gospels needs to be told, that against no evil in religious life did Jesus so often or so urgently warn His followers as against hypocrisy. 'The leaven of the Pharisees,' He called it; meaning by that emblem, as I suppose, to lay stress both on its slight and unobserved beginnings, and on its rapid and certain increase wherever tolerated. There is no guarantee for the purity of spiritual service, but resolutely to repel every particle of insincerity or unreality. Only admit ever so little regard to what men will say of you—only pretend to be in the very least holier or better than you are; and not only is your inner life no longer a whole, true, transparent thing, but you have admitted a working principle of falsehood, the nature of which is to spread, and to spread fast. The eye once diverted from the Father in heaven, gets incapable of looking straight at our unseen

Witness; the ear once open to the murmur of human applause at one's side, forgets to listen for that voice of heavenly approval which only faith can hear; the piety which, however genuine, is flaunted as a robe to be admired, soon ceases to be more than a cloak of deceit; in short, the entrance of insincerity is like the letting in of waters,—it widens its own passage, and drowns the soul in perdition at last. 'Take heed,' therefore. Whatever we do, let us do it as in God's sight, Who sees in secret as well as in public; whatever we are before God alone, that we are to be in the presence of men—that, and no more. Affect not any feelings or desires; no, nor tricks of voice, nor devoutnesses of manner, which are not downright and true, else you have no reward of your heavenly Father. 'No reward,' says Jesus here, putting God's judgment on hypocrisy at its lowest; because here He would only warn against the first false step, and spoke to hearts which were as yet tender and loyal. Hear how He spoke, a little later, to men who had travelled far on the road of the hypocrite, and had come to hide behind their stage dress and painted mask of piety nothing but greed and cruelty and lust: 'Woe unto you, scribes and Pharisees, hypocrites! fools and blind! whited sepulchres! children of hell!

Margin: PART II. THE PRINCIPLE. Cf. 1 Tim. vi. 9. See Matt. xxiii. 13-33.

generation of vipers!' Such startling words of indignation—words that shiver and scorch like lightning—He never uttered, except against the men who affected religion for the sake of appearances. Let each Christian, therefore, guard as his best treasure that life in secret, that holy tremulous fear of God, that openness to His eye, that simplicity of regard for His will, that unaffected indifference to all spectators save Him, which is the very soul and breath of all true righteousness; for without that we may have what credit we will among men, or wear what garb of goodness we please, but we have neither honour nor reward at the hands of the secret-judging Father, Who trieth heart and reins.

FIRST APPLICATION:

TO ALMSGIVING.

Therefore, when thou doest [thine] alms, do not sound a trumpet before thee, as the hypocrites do in the synagogues and in the streets, that they may have glory of men. Verily I say unto you, They have their reward. But when thou doest alms, let not thy left hand know what thy right hand doeth: that thine alms may be in secret; and thy Father, Which seeth in secret, [Himself] shall reward thee [openly].—MATT. VI. 2–4.

ALMSGIVING.

O F the three religious exercises to which Jesus applied His general warning against a hypocritical courting of publicity, almsgiving is undoubtedly the one with reference to which we moderns have most need to be warned. At the same time, it is the one which has now-a-days the least connection with the religious service of God. Since Christianity has succeeded in breathing a general spirit of compassion for the destitute and suffering into modern European life, and since society has been taught to respect the duty of beneficence on that broad ground of humanity which Christianity was the first to enforce, almsgiving, or rather all active charity from man to man, has ceased to be, to the same extent as formerly, an act of religion. It is no longer confined to religious persons. It is not so exclusively urged on religious grounds. Many who do not profess to be serving God in it, are ready enough to put their hand to enterprises of practical beneficence. It is, in fact, a virtue much

PART II.

FIRST APPLICATION.

PART II.
FIRST APPLICATION.

petted by that section of society which does not call itself religious, by whom it is usually opposed, either to the zeal of orthodoxy, which attaches weight to men's theological beliefs, or to that 'unpractical' piety which seeks to save people's souls while their bodies remain unrelieved. However idle or unjust this pitting of one virtue against another may be, religious persons have no reason to regret that the area of effective kindness among men has been much widened, or that one of the secondary fruits of Christ's faith has been to lead those who never would have shown any charity for God's sake, to show it for man's. Inadequate we must hold the merely humanitarian motive to be—inadequate at its best, and in the long-run unreliable, when not sustained by a deeper regard for His will Who is the Father of us all. Still we ought to rejoice when, from any motive whatever, the lot of our poor or ailing brothers is made lighter by generous hands. For the sake of our religion itself, however, it is of consequence that the intimate connection which it has so long had with benevolence should neither be forgotten nor relaxed. Charity has always been an integral part of practical Christianity; at the best of times it was even an offering of christian worship: and this sacred link between the service we pay to men and that which we owe to God is part of the good inheritance which Christianity drew from Judaism. The religious character attached to the duty of almsgiving, under both the earlier and the new economy, it will therefore be worth our while to trace.

PART II.

FIRST APPLICATION.

The Jewish commonwealth had no poor-law in the modern sense; but its legislation was skilfully directed, first to prevent poverty, and then to relieve in the kindest way such poverty as could not be prevented. The strange land-law which restored to its original owner, at the close of every half-century, all property[1] which, through pressure of misfortune, had become alienated, was a powerful instrument for preventing the accumulation of land in a few hands and the consequent growth of a hopelessly impoverished class. The general remission of outstanding debts at the same 'year of jubilee'[2] told in a similar direction. Still it was certain that the poor could 'never cease out of the land;' and the law enjoined on every Israelite the most generous

Deut. xv. 11.

---

[1] Except town property, or land devoted by its proper owner to sacred purposes. See Lev. xxv. 29–31, and xxvii. 18–24.
[2] See Josephus, *Antt.* iii. 12. 3.

<small>PART II.</small>

<small>FIRST APPLICATION.</small>
<small>Deut. xv. 1–4.</small>

<small>Lev. xxv. 5.</small>

<small>Deut. xiv. 28, 29, xxvi. 12–14.</small>
<small>Lev. xix. 9, 10, xxiii. 22.</small>

<small>Cf. Deut. xxiv. 19–22; Ruth ii. 2.</small>

<small>Deut. xvi. 10–17.</small>

consideration for his unfortunate brethren. He was urged to lend to the poor without interest, although debts of this character could not be recovered after the seventh year. Each seventh year, also, the spontaneous products of the untilled earth were open to any hand to pluck them; each third year one-tenth part of the crops was set aside, not, like the annual tithe, for the ordinary maintenance of the sacred tribe, but for special distribution among the destitute classes as well as among God's ministers;[1] each harvest the field corners were to be left designedly unreaped, and the smaller grape-clusters ungathered, that there might be something for the poor to glean; the standing crops were free to every hungry passer-by to eat; while, in order to connect the duty of charity closely with religion, the great religious festivals of the sacred year were celebrated with open banquets, at which, while the prosperous husbandman himself rejoiced over God's bounty, 'the stranger and the fatherless and the widow' were also to be welcome guests.

---

[1] There is some difficulty about the relation of these new prescriptions in Deuteronomy to the original tithe-law in Leviticus (xxvii. 30–33); but they are more likely to have been an addition to the annual tax than a limitation of it.

Throughout the whole of these most careful and liberal statutes, obedience was enforced by the highest of all considerations. It was because their fathers had been 'bondmen' and poor in Egypt, but had been redeemed by Jehovah's kindness; because the generous land they dwelt in was His land, and brought forth plenty at His bidding; because He loved to reward the merciful with increase, but was ready to avenge the cry of the needy; in short, it was because they 'feared God' that their eye was not to be 'evil,' nor their heart hard, nor their hand shut against their poor brother. This elevation of liberality to the poor into a sacred duty to God has naturally left its mark upon the whole later literature of the Hebrew people. Especially in the wealthy and relaxed age of Solomon do we find stress laid on alms as winning prosperity[1] and spiritual favour[2] from the Almighty; while the man who oppressed the poor by usury, or put them off with empty promises, was regarded as reproaching Him Who had made rich and poor alike, and in danger of forfeiting his unhallowed gains.[3] In spite, however, of both written laws and current maxims,

PART II.

FIRST APPLICATION.

Deut. xv. 15, xvi. 12, xxiv. 22.

Deut. xxiv. 14, 15, 19.

Cf. Deut. xv. 7-11.

---

[1] Cf. Prov. xiv. 21, xxii. 9, xxviii. 27.
[2] Prov. x. 2, xi. 4.
[3] See Prov. iii. 27, 28, xiv. 31, xvii. 5, xxii. 16, xxviii. 8.

PART II.
FIRST APPLICATION.

Isa. lviii. 6,7.

the bad times which followed in the disrupted kingdom were times of social wrong, and greed, and manifold oppression. The successive voices of the prophets are loud in their condemnation of the rich and powerful for 'grinding the faces' of their poorer countrymen, and 'selling the needy' for trifling gain.[1] When they summoned the land to repentance, this was the fast which the Lord chose: 'To deal thy bread to the hungry, and that thou bring the outcast poor to thy house; when thou seest the naked, that thou cover him; and that thou hide not thyself from thine own flesh.' Throughout the prophetic period, indeed, kindness to the poor is preached as one of the first duties of piety and a main proof of loyalty to their theocratic King Jehovah. It was evidently needed. Although we do not read of actual mendicancy till after the long captivity had shaken to pieces the old Mosaic institutions and utterly impoverished the land, there is no doubt that, under the later monarchy, luxury and injustice must have done their work, by reducing a large class to hopeless dependence upon charity; so that, more than ever, patriotism and religion

---

[1] Cf. amongst others, passages like Isa. iii. 14, 15; Jer. v. 28, xxii. 16, 17; Amos ii. 6, v. 11, 12, viii. 4–8; Ezek. xviii. 7–13; Zech. vii. 8–14.

Almsgiving.

combined to recommend to the pious an open-handed almsgiving.¹

Thus the Jewish mind was prepared for that exaggeration of this virtue which had come to prevail in the time of Christ, and which is one of the features of later Judaism. Already in the apocryphal books we find, along with excellent exhortations to liberality, an extravagant value ascribed to the exercise of it. 'Turn not thy face from any poor, and the face of God shall not be turned away from thee. If thou hast abundance, give alms accordingly; if thou have but a little, be not afraid to give according to that little: for thou layest up a good treasure for thyself against the day of necessity:' these are words which strongly recall what our Lord said about making heavenly friends out of the earthly mammon: but when it is added that 'alms do deliver from death' and 'shall purge away all sin,' or that 'alms maketh an atonement for sins' as water quencheth flame,² we feel that we are on

PART II.
FIRST APPLICATION.

Tob. iv. 7-11.

Luke xvi. 9; cf. xii. 33; Matt. xix. 21.
Tob. xii 9; Ecclus. iii. 30.

---

¹ Generosity to the poor is conspicuous in the Purim festivities (Esth. ix. 22), and in the rejoicings which celebrated the resumption of national worship in the rebuilt capital. Cf. Neh. viii. 10-12.

² This exaggeration of alms has been curiously revived in the Christian Church through the misinterpretation of the text, 'Charity shall cover the multitude of sins' (1 Pet. iv. 8). In

a soil out of which the fictitious righteousness of the Pharisees could grow. When such an exaggerated spiritual worth before God can be attached to any external act, were it the best a man can do, the spiritual sense must already have become distorted, and the way is prepared for the substitution of merely external acts for the inward spirit of righteousness.

This process of perversion had gone its full length when Jesus spoke. It is true that the arrangements for the collection of charity among the later Jews were admirable enough. A row of alms-boxes stood always in the temple court to receive the offerings of worshippers; at every Sabbath morning service in the synagogues, appointed officers collected money for the poor of the town, to be given away the same afternoon, besides a special offertory on fast-days; from house to house, also, agents solicited broken meats and other gifts for gratuitous distribution.[1] Through its times of deepest depression, the Jewish race has never since forgotten its old habit of remembering the poor. To this hour it

Marginal notes: PART II. FIRST APPLICATION. Cf. Mark xii. 41.

---

this, as in many other matters, debased Catholicism has run a similar course to debased Judaism.

[1] The authorities will be found cited by Winer in his *Real-wörterbuch*, under art. 'Almosen.'

sets to Gentiles and Christians a good example, and to this hour the ancient alliance between the worship of God and charity to the needy brotherhood has kept its ground. But the over-estimation of almsgiving, as a part of righteousness, corrupted the motives of it. Men who attach merit to the mere act, or fancy that parting with their money can of itself purchase forgiveness or reward from the Almighty, have already lost that spirit of humble gratitude to Him which chiefly makes the gift precious. That spirit gone, another inspiration will take its place. The good deed is performed, and the gift given, whatever motive lie behind it. Why should not reputation on earth, as well as favour from heaven, be the reward of so virtuous an action? To please God by doing alms, and please men by letting them see the alms we do, is a successful stroke which pays a man doubly for his outlay. Only there is an unhappy tendency in all cases where a lower motive mingles with a better one, that the base should by degrees eat away the noble. Neither a simple regard to God, nor even a pure generosity to men, will long dwell in the heart along with an interested eye to profit or applause; so that the rich Pharisee, who begins by trumpeting his good deeds, ends by hardly seeking any higher reward than a reputation for generosity. The hypocrites whom our Lord censured took care to bestow their charity at the synagogues, where the beggars congregated about the door and the people passing by could see; or they paraded their bounty, by dispensing it along the narrow and crowded Oriental thoroughfares. They might about as well have literally 'blown a trumpet,' as their namesakes the stage-players did, to call idle bystanders to the spectacle. Not without a touch of caustic satire does Jesus add, 'Verily they have their reward.' Men do look on and praise; even if the shrewder should nod to one another or whisper a jest about trumpet-blowing, at least the indigent who take his coin dare not show that they see through the donor's motive, and there are sure to be persons thoughtless enough to credit him with exceptional piety and benevolence. The man who plays at almsgiving, therefore, has what he covets and courts. But see! Above there is another Witness, in Whose pure name the farce is played, and before Whose face the player must one day stand. Surely what He has seen in secret, He too shall then reward very openly[1] indeed; but

---

[1] Throughout this section of St. Matthew the reading of the received text, ἐν τῷ φανερῷ, is discredited by some recent critics,

it shall be with that unlooked-for reward in which 'all liars' have a part.

We are now, I think, in a position to see what was our Lord's attitude towards this duty of almsgiving, and how it passed from the Old to the New Testament. Here also He did not destroy, but fulfil. For, in the first place, He had not a word to say against that ancient association of active beneficence with religious worship and the fear of God which had honourably distinguished the historical institutions of His countrymen. Rather, by re-asserting that alms must be given as in God's secret sight, He replanted charity in its true soil of godliness. He has left it where the whole development of Hebrew thought had placed it, in one class with prayers and fasting, as an integral part of a devout man's righteousness. It is true that both His own example (Who had everything except silver and gold to give) and the spirit of His own teaching have widened for us the sphere of our active beneficence. Bare almsgiving is not now the only, nor even the chief, way in which it is open to us to relieve men's material wants, or cure the social disorder

PART II.

FIRST APPLICATION.
Rev. xxi. 8.

Matt. v. 17.

Luke viii. 3;
cf. Acts iii. 6.

---

but, as regards verses 4 and 6, on doubtful authority. At all events, the idea of a *public* retribution is amply sustained by such passages as Matt. x. 32, xxv. 31-46 ; Luke ix. 26, xii. 1, 2.

out of which want springs. Christian charity early gave itself, with a blessed inventiveness in well-doing, to the healing of the sick, the ransom of the slave, the burial of the dead, the teaching of the young, and the like gratuitous services to society. In our more complex life, the solution of economical and social difficulties is perhaps its noblest and most arduous field. But when Jesus commended the generous widow, who cast all her living into the poor's box, and set her forth as a pattern of benevolence, He both recognised alms as a fit channel for charity where no other or better can be found, and at the same time praised by implication all less simple efforts to relieve distress or lessen the sum of human need. Whether it be only a 'mite' of money spared by thrift out of a slender income, or the foundations endowed by men of fortune, or personal attendance on the helpless and aged, or surgical ingenuity abridging pain, or statesmanlike labour to make every worker a fair sharer in the profits of labour; all forms of what, for shortness, we may call 'almsgiving' are equally elevated under the christian system into a pious service, and linked to the fear and love of our heavenly Father. Jesus taught His first disciples to see in the poor, whom we have always with us, representatives of

Himself, in relieving whom we pay Him service, and thus gave a new christian reading to the good old Hebrew saying, that 'he that hath pity upon the poor lendeth unto the Lord.' The first act of the new-born Church was to abolish poverty among her own members by a systematic distribution of alms on an unprecedented scale. So long as christian communities were small and oppressed, and mainly recruited from the labouring and servile classes, it was only within the circle of christian disciples that charity could be shown; but such charity was always enforced by the most sacred and spiritual motives. The self-impoverishing grace of the Son of God, His love of His brethren unto death, the common sonship to God which made christian men brothers in a sense which was then new, the unity of the christian body, and the supreme example which God had given of the blessedness of giving; these were the fresh thoughts which in the early Church gave to the old duty of almsgiving a mighty impulse,—thoughts fetched all of them out of the very holiest mysteries of the christian faith. The new revelation of God supplemented those pious considerations which from the time of Moses had given strength to Hebrew kindliness; yet apostles were not above borrowing,

PART II.

FIRST APPLICATION.

Prov. xix. 17.

Acts iv. 32–35.

2 Cor. viii. 9; 1 John iii. 16, iv. 20–v. 2; Acts xx. 35.

that they might use anew, the old arguments. Paul pleads with Corinth, in words of Solomon's, that to scatter with a generous hand is the secret of the best increase; and the writer to the Hebrews speaks of beneficence, as Isaiah might have done, as a sacrifice with which 'God is well pleased.' The truth is, that the infixed as well as inbred selfishness of men has need to be plied with every variety of noble motive for being generous; only the motives with which Scripture plies us are never drawn from a sentimental humanity, but always from a divine faith. The Church had ample justification, if not in the letter, yet in the spirit, of the Word, for that very old and beautiful usage which, by soliciting for the poor the alms of the faithful as often as they come together to 'eat bread,' has enshrined this whole duty of beneficence at the very centre and sanctuary of christian devotion.

<small>PART II.

FIRST APPLICATION.
2 Cor. ix. 6–11; cf. Prov. xi. 24, 25.
Heb. xiii. 16; cf. Isa. i. 11–17.</small>

While Jesus thus carried over into His new kingdom the traditional association of all humane and liberal deeds with the service of God, He strove, by applying to almsgiving the law of secrecy, to reanimate it with the spirit of sincere and unaffected godliness. All the more because this holy work of ministering to the poor was, and ought to be, a devout tribute paid to Him Who makes the rich man His steward and the poor His care, ought a pure regard for Him, and not for human opinion, to lie at the bottom of it. It is a wretched thing to turn what is meant to be a passage of love betwixt the true heart and its God into a piece of petty ostentation. Secrecy in giving is the cure which Christ prescribed. It is true, indeed, that provided the heart be honest and keep God alone in view as its Spectator and Rewarder, it will matter nothing where the alms are given, or with what publicity. But it is equally certain that the presence of witnesses sets a trap for the weakness of human vanity, suggests the desire to be observed, and easily, almost inevitably, adulterates the motive. Extremely few people, and especially few wealthy people, are above the temptation to let their munificence be known, that they may win the present pleasure of being praised, as well as the hope of some less appreciable reward in the world to come. How much must this temptation be increased when the current mode of collecting alms compels men to bestow them in public; nay, when this appeal to vanity is deliberately employed by the agents of charity for the purpose of drawing from the vain

PART II.

FIRST APPLICATION.

rich a larger subscription! It is not too much to say, that this motive of ostentation is worked in the interest of some of our public charities on a system. Secretaries, collectors, and other organizers of benevolence, are apt to be held successful at their work in proportion as they can play skilfully on this infirmity of the benevolent, and, by humouring men's love of reputation, swell the society's list. There is undoubtedly a certain space left, after higher motives have got their due, for the play of such a secondary, but still harmless, motive as emulation. Between different public bodies this may fairly be used in the service of charity. Paul was not ashamed to press liberality on the wealthy church at Corinth by the example of poorer Christians in Macedonia. Even emulation, however, is hardly a safe motive to work when individuals, not bodies of men, are to be handled; and it is nobleness itself, compared with the petty consideration of personal vanity. Who does not know that some men never contribute unless the donation is to be advertised in the papers? Are people never found to follow the lead of a few first subscribers, and give where aristocratic patrons have shown the way? Is it desirable that, when people are warm with wine, they should hear their offerings shouted forth at

PART II.
FIRST APPLICATION.

2 Cor. viii.
ix. passim.

the close of a charity dinner? Or what shall be said of firms the names of which figure prominently when a public subscription list is opened in the City, but for whose less obtrusive bounty no beggared family of orphans or broken-down clerk in their own office was ever much the better? Nor is the Church quite safe from a similar reproach; still less what is termed 'the religious world.' There are christian congregations where a bag handed round the pews will produce twice as much as an unobtrusive box in the porch. Missionary societies live to some extent by the same arts of canvassing, puffing, and advertising which are used for hospitals and orphanages. Our larger christian enterprises are usually started by published, and by no means anonymous, lists. I am far from meaning, of course, that it is always possible even for the most modest and sincere giver to escape such methods of giving; or that those who have great schemes of benevolence in hand can all at once shake themselves clear of the offensive features in our present system. But while there unquestionably is in England a vast amount of honest, good-hearted kindness, and of genuine christian liberality, let any man who knows ask himself whether there is not also entwined with it a vast deal which is spurious, and which people know to be spurious. Let him ask whether, without these offerings of the baser sort, either our benevolent or our religious undertakings could thrive, or perhaps exist, as they do; and whether it is not a fact that our methods of collecting are sometimes intentionally constructed so as to angle for the offerings of vanity as well as for those of piety? One wonders what words of sarcasm, mounting into outspoken wrathful denunciation, He would address to our modern Pharisees, were He sent again to London Who was once sent of the Father to old Jerusalem. Not that even these were to be His most fearful words against the ostentation of charity. So long as He sat on the lowly sward of our earth, with the wide-armed bounty of His Father's sunshine gladdening the soil and air around Him, it was well that He should speak humanly—not severely—of our human foibles: 'Verily I say unto you, Ye have your reward.' Other words will become those regal lips when the King shall be seated on His white throne of celestial judgment, and before His awful face 'fearfulness shall surprise the hypocrites.'

There is no cure for this rottenness at the heart of charity but secrecy. 'When thou doest alms, let not thy left hand know what thy right hand doeth.' If it would be a reason for giving more than the fear of God or the love of man prompts you to give, do not even say to yourself, with a glow of self-approval, 'I have given alms.' Certain acts of piety, such as private prayer, do naturally court seclusion from every eye. Unfortunately, in charitable deeds, there must commonly be at least two parties privy to the action: the giver and the receiver. In any case, let no third witness be by, if you can help it; nay, let not even the receiver know who is the donor, if you can help it. Let us do our best to discourage and abolish the vicious system of trumpeted benefactions, of advertised lists, of alms wheedled by flattery out of close fists, of weak though benevolent souls tempted into corrupt motives and the giving which brings no reward. It was the Church which first taught society throughout Christendom this now fashionable virtue of charity. It is the Church which can alone teach that better way of giving in the simplicity and unconsciousness of a childlike regard for the heavenly Father, which will make our charity fragrant, and not an offence, to Heaven. To bring our benevolence under the breath of our godliness; to make our alms as real a part of devotion as our prayers; to do good secretly and for God's sake; to devote

PART II.
FIRST APPLICATION.

first to God and to our Lord Christ what we propose to bestow on the Father's needy children or on Christ's little brethren: it is thus that we shall best redeem our charities from contempt, and make them more worthy of reward than a theatrical performance to the blowing of the trumpet of vanity.

SECOND APPLICATION:

TO PRAYER.

And when thou prayest, thou shalt not be as the hypocrites are; for they love to pray standing in the synagogues and in the corners of the streets, that they may be seen of men. Verily, I say unto you, They have their reward. But thou, when thou prayest, enter into thy closet, and when thou hast shut thy door, pray to thy Father Which is in secret; and thy Father Which seeth in secret shall reward thee [openly].—MATT. VI. 5, 6.

SECOND APPLICATION: TO PRAYER.

MIDWAY betwixt the giving of alms to men and the fasting which chastens one's own flesh, stands that central and most vital act of the religious life which more than any other expresses the soul's relation to God.[1] Prayer belongs more exclusively than either fasting or alms to the worship of God; and of all the usual forms which divine worship takes, it appears to be the most inward and sacred to secrecy. The song by which praise rises on waves of harmony to heaven needs a concert of practised voices; sacred oratory by which men are taught or stirred to holiness depends on the sympathy of numbers, and requires at least the two or three in whom Jesus saw the rudiments of His Church; the sacraments, too, are essentially public acts: but every solitude becomes a house of prayer when the solitary worshipper realizes that it is a house of God. Here therefore most of all, everything should be real. All affectation of devoutness is

_{PART II.}
_{SECOND APPLICATION.}

Matt. xviii. 20.

Gen. xxviii. 16 ff.

---

[1] 'Eleemosyna, tanquam præcipuum officium erga proximum; oratio, erga Deum; jejunium, respectu nostri.'—BENGEL *in loc.*

offensive; but to affect to hold personal intercourse with God, to pretend that we are speaking alone with Him, when we are doing no such thing but only inviting other men to hear us repeat a prayer, is unspeakably offensive. This is to thrust our insincerity under the very eye of the God of truth; to call His special attention to a farce; to add profanity to falsehood.

It may have been because prayer belongs so characteristically to the spiritual and personal side of the life of faith, and is of its own nature so free and jealous of prescriptions, that, among the minute regulations by which Mosaic law ordered all other parts of Hebrew worship, there occur no instructions for either the public or the private petitions of the people.[1] Yet the records of Old Testament saints are full of proofs that even under that economy of localized national worship, as at all other periods, religious life found its expression abundantly in unrestrained private petitions; while the prayer of King Solomon at the dedication of the temple amply shows that (with or without unrecorded directions from the Mosaic time) individual as well as national requests were habitually presented to Jehovah before His secret shrine and at the

---

[1] So Braune, quoted by Stier, *Reden Jesu*, in loc.

central seat of His people's worship. In the earliest periods, no set times for private prayer were probably observed, nor any other hallowed place frequented but the one national sanctuary. One of the Davidic psalms, however, speaks of praying in the evening, in the morning, and at noon. By the time of the long captivity, we find that the habit of private prayer thrice a day, at stated hours, had become recognised. Traces of a still more frequent observance of the duty appear in one of the latest psalms. The introduction of synagogue worship, probably soon after the return from Babylon,[1] by providing a convenient place for retirement, naturally served to confirm the custom of saying all prayers in public, which in the rabbinical schools was at length worked into a system. To this prayer-system of later Judaism the hypocrisy condemned by our Lord came ultimately to attach itself.

In order to understand our Lord aright, it must be borne in mind that His words apply in the first place to personal or private prayer. It is possible that, in His time as well as later, the synagogues were open for public prayer meetings every Monday and Thursday, as well as on the

Marginalia: PART II. SECOND APPLICATION. Ps. lv. 17. Dan. vi. 10, 11. Ps. cxix. 164.

---

[1] See the *Art.* 'Synagogue' in Smith's *Bible Dictionary*.

PART II.
SECOND
APPLICATION.

Sabbath-day;[1] and ostentatious religionists who preferred to throng these meetings rather than to pray in private, certainly came within the scope of His rebuke. But the stated assemblies of the pious for common prayer could not seem censurable in the eyes of One Who was Himself accustomed to attend them. Besides this, however, the doors of the synagogue seem to have stood open, as to this day they commonly do,—as the doors of the mosque and of the Roman Catholic church stand open,—for the greater part of every day, not for public but for private devotion; and it was first of all the abuse of this otherwise convenient arrangement by hypocritical worshippers against which Jesus warned His followers. To the pious Jew, or the Jew who desired to be esteemed pious, custom prescribed the repetition of certain forms of prayer at least three times a day. Modesty and true devoutness would have chosen to observe these hours, whenever it was possible to do so, in the privacy of home; but the Pharisees deliberately left their own houses for the sake of being seen at statutory prayer time in the open synagogue. Nor was this all. The hour of worship might surprise a man when passing

---

[1] On these later Rabbinical arrangements, cf. Tholuck, *Bergpredigt* in loc.

on a needful errand along the street; and, without meaning any display, a very conscientious Jew might stop, and turning so as to face the holy temple, recite his devotions where passers-by could not fail to see him. All who know anything of the East know how usual is this practice among pious Mohammedans. But, as it happens to-day among Mohammedans,[1] so it happened then among Jews: publicity encouraged hypocrisy. Sanctimonious persons, who coveted a repute for sanctity, took care to be pretty frequently on the street, especially at its most conspicuous and busy corners, when the call to prayer came; that, with superfluous punctuality and an overdone appearance of devoutness, they might perform the appointed recitation to the admiration of beholders.

Nothing, of course, about the present religious habits or the public opinion of Western nations encourages or would even tolerate abuses like these. On the contrary, we have banished religion so much out of sight, that we can hardly conceive how such practices should ever have become current. Even in those communions which still invite the faithful to say their private prayers in

---

[1] Cf. on the evil repute which very devout Moslems have among their neighbours, Thomson's *Land and Book*, p. 25 (Lond. 1859).

PART II.
SECOND
APPLICATION.

church, I do not know that a hypocritical parade of piety is at all a common result. Certainly, Protestants cannot be fairly accused of frequenting prayer meetings for the purpose of attracting general attention. Here and there no doubt, in religious circles, a person may be found whose prominence as a leader in prayer is only a cloak to disguise the rogue; and some poor pensioners of the church may be tempted by the hope of relief to be very regular in their attendance on public worship. But, speaking generally, the temptation is more powerful at present to conceal than to parade such piety as exists among us. The christian boy, for example, at a public school; the shopman and domestic servant who share their room with several mates; the poor believer who finds no privacy in those dens which we call by courtesy the homes of the people: these are in far greater risk of offending Christ by not praying at all than by praying too conspicuously. We have more need to have pressed upon us that other law of confession which enters to limit and complement the law of secrecy.

Matt. x. 32, 33, and par.; Rom. x. 10.

At the same time, the error which lay at the root of Pharisaic ostentation in prayer is too subtle to be ever wholly banished, and the correction which our Lord supplied is too precious ever to be forgotten. At the root of the abominable affectation which vitiated the prayers of many among His contemporaries, lay, as I conceive, this mistake: That instead of regarding prayer as a spontaneous childlike utterance of dependance upon God, which has no value in itself, but only as a medium of intercourse; men had come to reckon prayer among the constituent acts of a man's righteousness, pleasing or meritorious for its own sake in the eyes of Heaven. From speaking in these verses of hypocritical saying of prayers, Jesus diverges in those which follow to the parallel abuse of superstitious repetition of prayers. That is strictly an *excursus* from the main thought of the present section; but both abuses spring from the same source. It is one blunder respecting the nature of prayer and where its value lies, that led the Pharisees, as it always has led men, both to praying which is superstitious and to praying which is hypocritical; to prayers by rote and prayers for show. The Jew who, like a heathen, recited over and over again the same words, did so because, like a heathen, he had come to attach merit or value to the mere act of praying. Prayer, that is to say, had become in his eyes, no longer a simple request addressed by a child to his Father, useful only as

<small>PART II.

SECOND APPLICATION.

Vers. 7, 8.</small>

it carried to the Father the child's desire; but a work of religion, a good action, itself prescribed as a test or sign of godliness, the performance of which would operate, if not as a charm, at least as a merit, to win by its acceptableness the blessing of God. For this reason, he prayed very often and very long; for this reason also he prayed where men could see him pray. Prayer viewed as a soul's petition to God is of its own nature a private thing. Its value lies in its being heard and understood by Him. It craves no overhearing ear, for to other ears than His it carries no meaning and has no value. On the contrary, it rather shrinks from, than courts, the observation of any third party. So long as you only pray because you are in need, and because you cannot help telling God what it is you need, prayer continues to be an affair of two: it lies between the petitioner and the Giver. It is only when prayers have become services or acts of religion, by the number or the length or the regularity or the fervency of which a man makes himself pleasing to God and exhibits to men the quality of his piety, that there can arise the slightest temptation to take one's private devotions into public places or say them aloud for others to hear.

It is at this point that we discover the precise bearing of that corrective which our Lord supplied. To this central utterance of spiritual life, He applied His law of secrecy in religion. Here, if anywhere, that law is in its place. As all religious acts, to be worth anything, must have God for their sole spectator, so eminently must this act, which is the very heart of our religion, be done in secret. The true type of all prayer therefore is solitary prayer. Its favourite resort is not the synagogue, but the closet. It is, to go to the essence of the thing, just a word spoken to that Father Whose characteristic is that He is most with us when we are in secret, and is felt to see us there most closely where no one else can see us. But a word of request simply spoken to God alone never can be construed into a meritorious performance or exalted into a department of human 'righteousness.' To drive prayer back behind a shut closet door is to revive the true conception of it and to cut off occasion from both these later misgrowths, the public saying of prayers, which is ostentation, and the idle repeating of prayers, which is superstition.

I have said that it is with private, not social, prayer our Lord is here dealing. The abuses He corrects were abuses which clung less to the public

PART II.
SECOND
APPLICATION.

than to the individual worship of His countrymen. It is our personal intercourse with God which He expressly banishes from open gaze into the closed chamber. No inference, therefore, to the discouragement of family or social or congregational worship can legitimately be drawn, or by any reasonable men ever has been drawn, from His words. In strict truth, however, even social prayer, in which many worshippers unite in one petition, remains subject to the same law of secrecy. No two or more Christians have any better right than a single Christian has to stand and perform their devotions in a conspicuous place, for the purpose of attracting the attention of those who are not worshippers.[1] The ordinary rule of social as well as of personal prayer is, that it be more or less concealed from mere spectators, never obtruded on their notice, least of all performed for their admiration. The place of prayer may be vast as a cathedral; but the congregation is presumed to be alone. The worshippers have but one heart, as well as one voice. A common

---

[1] I do not mean, of course, to reflect upon the efforts of street preachers to gain an audience for the gospel, by singing or praying at street corners; because these are to be justified by quite other considerations. They contemplate a very different end from the admiration of non-worshipping bystanders. They aim at turning bystanders into worshippers.

desire makes of many petitioners one petitioner. No one's attention is distracted by the presence of a single onlooker. The people bow in their great house of prayer just as each man bows in his little closet, before Him Who still is seeing in secret. Not he who reverently joins his desire with the desire of his fellows; but he who while professing to pray with his neighbours allows himself to become a mere spectator of his neighbour's prayer: he it is who really violates the privacy of the House of God.

After all, then, it is the closet, and not the church, which is the primary or typical oratory. Spiritual life never continues to be individual only; it becomes also social: but it is individual first of all. It is born in the secrecy of the soul; it is nurtured in the secrecy of the closet. Constituted as men are, it is impossible to be in the presence of others so absolutely unconscious of witnesses, so perfectly spontaneous, so unaffectedly true, as we may be where only God can see us. To know how far the devotional feeling of which we are conscious in social worship is genuine, it is needful to carry it into the cool, hushed, and lonely presence-chamber of the secret Father, and submit it there to the scrutiny of His testing eye and of our own. The habit of worshipping exclusively in the presence of even the nearest and most congenial of fellow-Christians—supposing it possible for a Christian—would put in peril the integrity and simplicity of any man's religion. It would beget an evil consciousness of self at the most solemn moments of life. It would hinder religious emotion from penetrating beneath the surface, and by keeping it dependent on the sympathy of others, would degrade it into a sentiment. It would tempt him to look more to the form than to the spirit of his worship. It would be apt to confuse the singleness of his regard to God, as the Witness, no less than the Object, of his adoration. Above all, it would interfere with the outspokenness and utterly unreserved frankness with which each child of God should address his heavenly Father. Religion may be said to commence when a soul ceases to keep back any secret from God. To live always bare to the soul's core in His sight is the condition of healthful religion. To speak out in His ear what cannot be spoken in another's—those incommunicable things which only each man's own spirit knows, and which can be told even to God only in such inarticulate groans as need a divine Interpreter: this is that manner of praying which is a necessity in the religious life, and which

[marginal note: 1 Cor. ii. 11; c. Rom. viii. 26.]

can only be reached in secret. The reason for this necessity runs down into that mysterious personality which makes every human being at the last resort a solitude, impervious to his fellow, accessible only to his God. Largely indeed it is with sin, the peculiar consciousness of which each man takes to be an unparalleled and incommunicable experience of his own; with sin, and with the secret struggle he has to make against it, that the solitary confessions and petitions of a Christian must for the present be occupied. Yet this necessity for solitary prayer is so far from resting on the evil state of man that it is rather found to increase as men make progress toward perfection; while the memorable example of our Lord Himself, throwing back light upon His words, demonstrates how indispensable even to a perfect Son of God was such retirement from human sight into the solitary presence of His Father.

This retreat therefore from all human presences back into that One Presence where we can be nakedly ourselves, and can breathe all secrets into an ear which perfectly understands, and lean all weakness upon a bosom which perfectly loves; this retreat which Jesus Himself was forced on several occasions to seek by night on a lonely hill or in an orchard, is not only the sweetest

PART II.

SECOND APPLICATION.

Cf. Mark i. 35; Luke vi. 12; Matt. xiv. 23, xxvi. 36; and their parallels.

luxury of genuine spiritual life, but its supreme necessity. The place to which a man may retire to be with God is of such inferior moment that in case of need any place will answer. To be literally without human companionship or the risk of observation is no doubt most desirable. Among the numerous evils which spring from the overcrowding of both the urban and the rural poor into insufficient dwellings, the absence of a private room, or at least of a noiseless and undisturbed corner for prayer, is not to be overlooked. In the country, to be sure, one can generally walk alone, like Isaac, in the fields; but it is hard to see what retreat from intrusion is left to the pent-up city poor, whose wretched lodgings do not even boast that store-room with a door to it which Jesus took for granted might be found in any ordinary Jewish home.[1] If it were not too entire a departure from English habits, one would be tempted to wish that our churches in crowded localities could be utilized on week-days for private prayer, or else some smaller and more

Part II. Second Application.

Gen. xxiv. 63.

---

[1] The word rendered 'closet' is not that by which the 'upper room,' or guest-room, of a Jewish house is commonly indicated (ὑπερῷον), but ταμεῖον (or ταμιεῖον), rendered 'storehouse' in Luke xii. 24, and 'secret chamber' in Matt. xxiv. 26. It probably is purposely general, and signifies any small or subsidiary room not usually employed for living in.

secluded oratories provided, to which weary souls might retire at a spare moment, in search of that peace and spiritual refreshment which must be sought in vain where the voices of boisterous neighbours are always audible through the frail partition, and the tiny strip of domestic floor room must serve the ends at once of kitchen and of nursery. It is quite beyond any one's power to estimate how far this mere want of opportunity for retirement is daily operating to drive all religious reflection and private prayer out of the lives of thousands of our English poor. What is so excessively inconvenient is sure to be treated by most people as a practical impossibility. At the same time, it is never really impossible to be alone with God. To be silent and to think, always means to be alone. The seclusion which we may make within our own bosom is a closer solitude than that of bolted doors.[1] And the soul that has once pushed its way with struggle and pain through that guilty silence which like a wall holds back the impenitent from the face of God, and has once tasted the inexpressible deliciousness of being confidential with its reconciled Father;

---

[1] So some of the Fathers, as Origen and Augustine, expounded the 'closet;' but a literal removal into solitude must be intended, where it is practicable.

PART II.
SECOND APPLICATION.

that soul must and will again and again make for itself times and places and methods for getting back into sweet colloquy with the secret Author of its life, with the only One before Whom it has nothing to conceal, and from Whom it has everything to hope.

Our Father Who is in secret loves to be the one privileged Intimate of each heart among His children. In the preference for Him which forces a man to be dissatisfied with all meaner company; in the trustfulness which dares to tell Him everything; in that self-asserting irrepressible instinct of childship which must cry out to its unseen Father, though philosophy should dissuade, and reason should lose its way in its effort to justify the cry: in all this the paternal Heart on high finds such delight as paternal hearts below would find; and each low breathing which goes up unseen from any tender tearful penitent or from a warm affectionate worshipper, goes, like a sigh from some heart of little child too fond to speak, straight unto the Father.

He shall reward it, said the Son of His love. But I trust we know that He doth reward it; not 'openly' indeed, nor always by manifest accomplishment of such things as our ignorance may solicit; never perhaps in such ways as can be tabulated in our statistics; yet is His response none the less certain, because it is as secret as our prayer was secret, felt only by the instinct of love, and given only to the heart of the child. So surely as he who hath been born of God must have that to say unto his Father which can be spoken in no other ear, so surely shall the great Father make such answer within His child as it is not given to any stranger to surmise. There are more things passing betwixt heaven and earth than are dreamt of in our philosophy; and divine love, like the earthly, has secrets of its own. Wouldst thou know them for thyself? Then 'enter into thy closet, and when thou hast shut thy door,' learn there how to 'pray to thy Father Which is in secret;' for thee also 'thy Father Which seeth in secret shall reward.'

EXCURSUS:

THE MODEL PRAYER.

But when ye pray, use not vain repetitions, as the heathen do: for they think that they shall be heard for their much speaking. Be not ye therefore like unto them: for your Father knoweth what things ye have need of, before ye ask Him. After this manner therefore pray ye: 'Our Father, Which art in heaven! Hallowed be Thy Name: Thy kingdom come: Thy will be done in earth as it is in heaven: Give us this day our daily bread: And forgive us our debts, as we forgive our debtors: And lead us not into temptation, but deliver us from evil: [For Thine is the kingdom and the power and the glory for ever, Amen].' *For if ye forgive men their trespasses, your heavenly Father will also forgive you: but if ye forgive not men their trespasses, neither will your Father forgive your trespasses.*—MATT. VI. 7–15.

Cf. LUKE XI. 1–4.

EXCURSUS: THE MODEL PRAYER.

BEFORE leaving the subject of prayer, to apply His law of secrecy to fasting as the third constituent in Hebrew 'righteousness,' Jesus turns aside from His rebuke of hypocrisy to forbid another abuse, no less inconsistent with the true idea of worship. Superstition is a disease as inveterate in every false religion as hypocrisy is in the true. But although it has always attached itself by preference to heathen faiths, there is enough of native heathenism in every human heart to develop superstitious practices even in the worship of the true God. Degenerate Judaism, like degenerate Christianity, had its occasional paganism. The notion that God is a Being Who can be wrought upon by the mechanical iteration of petitions till they become wearisome, was indeed too foreign from the spiritual monotheism of Israel ever to become popular. From the earliest instance in Scripture of vain repetition, when Baal's Phœnician priests called on his name from morn till noon, down to the latest, when

PART II.

EXCURSUS.

1 Kings xviii. 26.

Diana's votaries at Ephesus shouted out her greatness 'about the space of two hours,' it is on heathen ground that we find it flourish. The fact, however, that Hebrew teachers of various ages found it needful to warn their countrymen against it, suggests that devout Jews must often have betrayed some tendency to fall into this error. The truth is, that, as we have seen, it has at bottom the same root as hypocrisy. A religion of forms, such as the Pharisees practised, runs very readily into a religion of charms, such as pagans believe in. When the Pharisee recited his 'long prayer' in order to appear devout, his prayer was only said, not prayed. Whatever trust he placed in its efficacy, therefore, was likely to rest, not on its sincerity, but on its length or frequency; and the more he expected from his devotions, he would be only the more apt to rely upon the reiteration of them. Forms of prayer, which, in order to please men, had been at first repeated as a pretence, would thus come to be repeated, in order to please God, as a charm. In either case prayer became a vain thing: only its vanity was in the one case the vanity of falsehood; in the other, the vanity of folly. Betwixt these two poles, all false religion for ever vibrates.

For both hypocritical and superstitious prayers,

the remedy is similar. A just conception of what prayer is as the offering up of childlike desire to One Who is in secret, will always save us, if we are faithful to it, from saying our prayers 'for a pretence.' A just conception of His character to Whom our prayers are offered, will equally save us from saying them as an incantation. The heathen 'think that they shall be heard for their much speaking,' because they have a heathenish notion of the Divine Being. They suppose Him to be ignorant of their need till He is told; disinclined to help them till He is importuned; capricious, so that He must be humoured; or indolent, so that He can be pestered into compliance. It is nothing else but a parallel mistake as to the nature of God which is made by those ignorant Christians who dutifully repeat every day certain formal petitions which express no real desire, or mumble over the same form of prayer scores of times without stopping, under the belief that such a mechanical style of worship is pleasing to the Eternal. Surely it is no less unworthy of the Father to fancy that He can be gratified by empty phrases which mean nothing, or that He will find some merit to reward in the pattering of beads, than it would be to attract His attention by shouting or win

PART II.

EXCURSUS.

Cf. *Obtundere Deos*: Terence.

His favour by self-laceration, like the priests of Baal. To 'acquaint' oneself with the true God is here, as in so many things, to 'be at peace.' Jesus discloses the Father to us; and our worship becomes rational by becoming filial. Our Father knows before we speak what it is that we would have, and before we are willing to ask, He is ready to bestow. He needs neither to be informed, nor to be coaxed, nor to be wrought upon. He waits indeed for the voice of His child to be lifted up in a lowly sense of want, with earnest desire for a gift; and that the child may be led to lift up a voice of prayer, the Father may often find it meet to leave its sore need for a while unfilled: but He neither waits for, nor can be in the least moved by, anything else.

Of course, this true and perfect fatherliness in God, while it condemns as futile all repetition merely for speaking's sake, does not condemn, but, on the contrary, encourages, the importunity of earnest and even passionate longing. He to Whom we pray knows us too well and loves us too much to be displeased when the overfull heart of His child cannot content itself with few or cold words, said once and said no more; but like the Son in the olive-yard, sends up petition on petition in spontaneous reduplication, mingled too with such 'strong crying and tears,' as though the soul would, with violence not to be gainsaid, besiege the very gate of heaven.[1] God has as little need to be importuned as He has to be informed; yet for the same reason that He would have us pray at all, would He have us pray with the fervency and frequency of an 'inwrought' desire. He who has no belief in God will not pray to Him at all. He who has some misshapen belief in Him as other than He is, may use prayer as a meritorious or a magical instrument for the securing of benefits. But the christian man, who trusts in the perfect knowledge and kindness of God as his Father, and who knows that prayer is nothing but the unfettered spontaneous utterance in his Father's ear of all that the soul, when blown upon by the breath of God, can feel or wish, will neither force himself to repeat prayers when he desires nothing, nor restrain himself from any fashion of praying or continuance in it, which is prompted by genuine emotion. He Who inspires desire, may well be trusted to understand and to excuse its utterances.

PART II.
EXCURSUS.

Jas. v. 16, Greek.

---

[1] To the point are Augustine's words, quoted by Meyer, *in loc.* : Absit ab oratione multa locutio, sed non desit multa precatio, si fervens perseveret intentio.

PART II.
EXCURSUS.

Luke xi. 1, 2.

It was, in the first instance, as a pattern of what our prayers ought to be, if we would avoid this fault of heathenish repetition, that our Lord here introduced the form which we are accustomed to call by His name. On a subsequent occasion, indeed, mentioned by St. Luke, He showed that He had designed it to be used for a liturgy, as well as a model; since, when His followers begged that He would do as the Baptist and other Jewish masters had done—would teach them words to pray in, He dictated substantially the same petitions which He had given in the Sermon on the Mount, and bade them repeat these when they prayed. We have therefore ample warrant for either the public or the private employment of the very words of this divine liturgy, as often as in our prayers we feel our need of such assistance. We shall also be justified, I think, in taking its petitions to be a divine directory for all prayer. Our Lord can hardly have intended to restrict His rubric, 'After this manner pray ye,' to mean only, After this manner of brevity and simplicity in style; but also, After this manner of thought and desire. When Jesus did by us as we do by the little ones—put (so to say) our hands together, and bade us look up into the sky and say after Him in simple phrase, 'Our Father, Which art in Heaven;' He could not but set us an example as perfect in the matter, as it is in the manner, of it.

In the first instance, however, it is to the form rather than to the contents of this model, that the connection compels our attention. Because our christian prayers are not to be like those of heathens, 'therefore' we are to order them after the fashion of this standard. That must mean, that our prayers are to be brief, direct, comprehensive, orderly, and real. Very brief is the model He sets, according to that word of Solomon's: 'God is in heaven, and thou upon earth; therefore let thy words be few.' The youngest memory is not burdened to retain these 'few words.' Each clause is perfect in terseness, stripped bare of every word not indispensable, and looks alongside our overloaded devotional phraseology like the skeleton of a prayer. There is absolutely no repetition; the petitioner moves at once from each naked but weighty request to the next. How direct, too, is every word! As though the suppliant kept silence till he quite clearly saw what it was he needed to ask, and having simply asked for it without vagueness or circumlocution, was silent again. One feels as if a great pause ought to separate

PART II.

EXCURSUS.

Eccles. v. 2.

PART II.
EXCURSUS.

the several clauses; a pause to be filled up with calm thought and the preparation of the heart for a new request. It is from this background of reverent meditative silence that the petitions appear to go up at intervals—each one piercing heaven like an even-feathered arrow shot by a strong arm. In every clause, too, what a world of desire is shut up! No more than six requests, or seven at most;[1] yet though the words might be lisped by infant's lips, the whole wide round of human want and of christian desire is traversed and gathered up. Each clause might stand as the title to an entire chapter in the universal prayer-book of the Church; for under these half-dozen comprehensive head-lines you may range all the possible supplications, however varied, of God's vast christian family. The fulness of devotional longing condensed into each petition neither narrows the worshipper's horizon nor obscures his logical vision; for in this prayer, all those objects for which men ought to ask find a place, and each

---

[1] In the West, they have commonly been reckoned as six; in the East, as seven. Were it not for the ἀλλὰ in ver. 13, one could hardly be persuaded to treat so splendid a prayer as 'Deliver us from the evil' as only a repetition in more positive and general terms of the preceding words: 'Lead us not into temptation.'

its proper place. From things divine to things human, from temporal to spiritual need, the well-ordered sentences progress. Sober judgment keeps its hand even on the movements of devout emotion; and while nothing is forgotten, there is nothing overstrained. In a word, the most intense reality characterizes this model of prayer; arising from the concentration of a man's whole nature—intellect, spirit, and purpose—all bent to know what things are the most desirable, and, with childlike straightforwardness and such absorption as renders the petitioner unconscious of others, to beg those things from the Father in heaven. 'After this manner, therefore, pray ye.'

When from its form we pass to the contents of the Lord's Prayer, still carrying in our hand as a clue this ruling thought, that it is the type upon which all prayers are in their own way to be modelled, we find it still more full of teaching.

1. The invocation, by the name which it gives to God and the terms in which it teaches us to address Him, gives the key-note of christian supplication. It is for this reason the most distinctively christian part of the whole. The six petitions, if not all borrowed (as the first and

second of them are said to be [1]) from rabbinical forms of prayer which may be as old as Jesus' day, are at least conceived in a Hebrew quite as much as in a christian spirit. They are too catholic to wear any novel or peculiar colour. They belong to the new dispensation, but to that part of it which it shares with the old. They are in place on christian, but not out of place on Jewish, lips. The doxology, on the other hand, which appears to have been added, in the East at least, at a very early date,[2] in order to adapt the prayer to liturgical use in the public worship of the Church, is so Jewish in its form that it may have been, or probably was, condensed from the words with which King David blessed Jehovah on the day of his successor's coronation. Had it been desired to append some concluding clause which should express the natural response of every christian heart to all those requests which Jesus here puts into the Christian's mouth, the appropriate phrase

---

[1] For the evidence of this, see references in Tholuck, Grotius, and others.

[2] The authority of the best MSS. (Vat., Sin., D, etc.) compel us, I fancy, to reject the doxology from the text, as Tischendorf, Olshausen, Meyer, Tholuck, and most modern scholars do. Its absence in all the Latin Fathers showed that it can only have gained a late currency in the Western Church. On the other hand, it is found in the Syriac Peschito, supposed to date from the second century.

would have been one bearing on the mediatorial propitiation and advocacy of Jesus Himself. No express allusion to this could be appropriate, so long as Jesus stood within the confines of the Hebrew dispensation—His work of atonement unaccomplished, and the Spirit Who should inaugurate the new economy not yet given. But from the beginning of her history, the instincts of the Christian Church must have supplied that unexpressed basis on which all acceptable prayer now takes its stand, since we have been taught that no man cometh unto the Father but by the Son. For the characteristic christian tone of this prayer, therefore, we must look to the invocation alone. What neither the body of the prayer nor its conclusion does, is virtually done for it by its opening words. It was Jesus Christ Who revealed God to be 'Our Father in heaven;' and it is the disciples of Jesus Christ who are entitled on the ground of regeneration and adoption to address Him by that name. For though in some few scattered texts of the Old Testament the peculiar relation of the Israelitish people to Jehovah had been expressed under the image of paternity,[1] yet it was our Lord Who first adopted

PART II.

EXCURSUS.

Matt. x. 5, 6,
xv. 24; Rcm.
xv. 8; John
vii. 39.

John xiv. 6.

---

[1] Deut. xxxii. 6 is the seed-text in this connection. Compare Isa. lxiii. 16, lxiv. 8; Jer. iii. 4, 19, xxxi. 9; and Malachi i. 6.

this name of 'Father' as the one proper name under which alone He Himself knew or ever spoke of Him from Whom He had come. So exclusive was Jesus' employment of the word as His own name for God, that it could not but awaken attention when He habitually encouraged His followers also, and none but His followers,[1] to think of the Most High as their Father too. It was only by receiving Jesus as the Son of God, by believing on Him as the image of the Father, and by becoming one with Him, that the disciples of Jesus learned to address the Eternal, as they are here taught to do, under this endearing name. There is a great deal more of loving and confiding

---

Jehovah called Himself a Father with special reference to David, in the promise of 2 Sam. vii. 14 (1 Chron. xvii. 13), to which Ps. lxxxix. 26, 27 refers. The comparison in Ps. ciii. 13 bears only on one aspect of the relationship, and can hardly be included in this short list, which comprises, I think, all the passages of this class in the Old Testament. The use of the word in this connection became more frequent and explicit after the close of the Hebrew canon: cf. Ecclus. xxiii. 1; Tobit xiii. 4; Wisdom xiv. 3; and especially the remarkable passage in the latter book: ii. 12–20. In our Lord's time, it was the boast of the nation that God was its Father; see John viii. 41.

[1] A comparison of the passages in the Evangelists (s. Bruder, *s. v.* πατήρ) in which our Lord spoke of God as '*your Father*' will show that, without one exception, He was addressing, not a mixed audience, but His own disciples. The passages are (besides those in this Sermon on the Mount and its parallels): Matt. x. 20, 29, xiii. 43, xviii. 14, xxiii. 9, Mark xi. 25, and John xx. 17.

familiarity in such a form of address than we should have dared of ourselves, either as creatures or as criminals, to cherish. It is the Eternal Son, Who, having brought us near by the blood of His cross and begotten us again by His Spirit, leads us by the hand to the bosom of infinite love, and encourages us, not as though we were exceptional favourites, but as members of a reconciled family,[1] to whisper the sweetest of names. At the same time, it is the peculiarity of this filial affection that it joins with such familiarity the lowliest and most submissive reverence. He Who has here taught us to lift our eyes to the lofty place where our Father dwells was the most reverential of men. In the blending of these two feelings which this invocation suggests—of the love which draws boldly near, and the awe which restrains from over-boldness—lies the just temper of all christian prayer. Our prayers may be at one time more intimate, and at another more distant, according as the heart is touched. At one time, the worshipper may feel with greater force that he is a son, and at another that his Father is in heaven. What is essential is that intimacy should never

---

[1] This seems to be employed in the plural pronoun 'Our.' At the same time, this was customary in Jewish forms of prayer even when designed for private use.

degenerate on the one side into the audacity of disrespect, nor awe grow on the other to faithless and unfilial fear. And this golden mean will always be observed, so long as the spirit of all christian prayer shall answer the model invocation: 'Our Father Which art in heaven.'

2. The division and arrangement of the petitions point further to the spirit which ought to rule our christian desires. Jesus teaches us to pray in a noble, disinterested, and godly way. Before He suffers us to descend to those requests which touch our personal wants, even the most urgent, He lifts our hearts, as the hearts of children ought to be lifted, into sympathy with the larger purposes of our Father in heaven. In obedience to His own rule (to be laid down a little later), He sets us out of ourselves into a divine unselfishness, and bids us 'seek first the kingdom of God and His righteousness' before we ask any of those other things which require to be added unto us. The first place in our desires, like the first table of our duty, belongs to God. That the world should be brought to recognise, as God's children have learned to do, the awful sanctity and separate incommunicable majesty of His revealed character as Christ has declared it to us, so as to feel its own sins against the Holy One and peni-

tently return to a practical acknowledgment of God; that the true theocracy, or divine rule over the earth, foretold in Hebrew Scriptures, should be universally set up by the exaltation of God's Anointed King and the submission of all men to His spiritual control; and that, as the consummation of this saving process, rebellion should die out of the earth, and every human will, brought back to its allegiance, should move once more in free and glad obedience to that supreme Will which sways unfallen and celestial spirits: this threefold desire for the success of God's work of restoration, in its beginning, middle, and end, is to be the foremost passion of every child of God, as it is the Father's own abiding and most cherished purpose. So distinctly did Jesus rebuke by anticipation that subtle selfishness in religion which cares for itself first, and only in the second place for God's honour or authority. It is to be remembered indeed that this is a prayer for men already reconciled to God; and therefore it cannot be applied without modification to the case of the unregenerate, whose foremost duty, as well as most urgent interest, it must always be to repent and call upon the name of the Lord that they may be saved. So far as they are concerned, this is the one way in which the divine Name needs

Acts ix. 21; Rom. x. 13; quoted from Joel ii. 32.

in the first instance to be hallowed and the divine Kingdom to come. It is to be expected that a man who has once been lifted into the fellowship of Christ will be free to consider wider interests. To pray for one's own individual wants as if there were no greater or more clamant need beneath the sun, is not to be like Jesus. The Christian who looks abroad with eyes like those of a son of God will see one tremendous want on earth which dwarfs every personal consideration. That everywhere among men God's name is profaned, God's rule defied, God's will broken; this is that sight which the soul of God's child will soonest cry out for: and when admitted into the presence-chamber to lay at God's feet whatever weighs most heavily on his heart, this will be the cry which rises soonest to his lips, that the dishonoured Father be once more revered, the Father's disowned supremacy restored, and the Father's broken orders again obeyed.

3. Another point in which this model prayer is exemplary is in the place it assigns to temporal blessings. Against the overdriven spirituality which affects to be too indifferent to earthly good to think it worth asking for, Jesus vindicates a place for it in our prayers.[1] But against the

---

[1] To this overdriven spirituality we must set it down, when

worldliness which would prostitute prayer into a mere instrument for averting material disaster or securing material benefit, Jesus has restricted our desires to the most modest necessaries. It is not inconsistent with that trustful dependence on the spontaneous bounty of Him, Whose open hand feeds the birds of the air, of which Jesus goes on by and bye to speak, that we should be permitted to solicit what is needful for the life of to-day, or even a bare provision against to-morrow.[1] Rather, it is the most natural and becoming expression of that hand-to-mouth dependence (if I may so express it). For the poor man, it is good that he is encouraged to lay even this mean but gnawing care of his heart before the great House-Father, lest he should be tempted to distrust of providence. For the rich man, it is no less good that he should be reminded of the insecurity of earthly abundance and made a beggar at the gate of God, not for wealth, but for food. But there is no encouragement to be got

PART II.

EXCURSUS.

See Matt. vi. 25–34.

Olshausen reads even this petition in a spiritual sense. See his Commentary *in loc.*

[1] There is much to be said for the derivation of that difficult word ἐπιούσιος, which our version renders 'daily,' from ἡ ἐπιοῦσα. In that case we should read, 'Give us to-day our bread for to-morrow.' The rendering 'daily' is in any case extremely doubtful.

from these words for the habit of importuning God for such success, prosperity, or immunity from trial as God has not promised, and may send, if He send it at all, for a temptation or a penalty.

4. The last lesson of this prayer which I shall mention is of such special moment and so hard to learn, that our Lord Himself has called attention to it, by what may be termed a note of explanation appended to the fifth petition. That the divine forgiveness is conditioned by a forgiving temper in the suppliant was not a new thought to the hearers of this Sermon; for it is the subject of one of those Beatitudes with which the Sermon opened. But it was a favourite point in our Lord's teaching: and we nowhere find it put with greater emphasis or earnestness than in the words appended to this prayer. That it is even embedded in the texture of the prayer itself; that where brevity was so much studied as here, Jesus could not teach us to say, 'Forgive us our debts,' without bidding us add in the same breath, 'as we forgive our debtors;' suggests how absolute is this condition of our pardon and how essential to be perpetually kept in mind. These words take for granted that we have already pardoned all offenders against ourselves before we pray, and are, as Jesus had already taught that

we should be, in peace with all men. If, however, any one should presume to present this petition to Almighty God with a resentful or implacable heart, then must we not say that it will turn in his mouth into a terrific petition against forgiveness? For then it will run thus, in the ear of God: Forgive not my debts, as I do not forgive my debtors. The truth is, the attitude of true prayer is *ipso facto* inconsistent with revenge or unmercifulness; for it assumes a prior repentance for sin, and a present sympathy with the mind of 'the Father of mercies,' both of which exclude the diabolic spirit of unforgiving anger.

PART II.

EXCURSUS.

2 Cor. i. 3.

To open up at length the comprehensive sense of each of these six petitions would require a chapter to be devoted to each.[1] All that is here demanded of us by the connection in which this model form occurs as an appendix to the present section of our Lord's discourse, is that we should try to gather up such general hints as it was intended to afford respecting the form, the matter, and the spirit of our own daily prayers. Much as it has been used by the Church, and often as it recurs in the family and social worship of devout

---

[1] In recent literature, this has been thoughtfully and elegantly done by Mr. Dods, in his '*Prayer that Teaches to Pray.*' (Edin. 1863.)

PART II.
EXCURSUS.

persons, it may be doubted whether its lessons as a teaching specimen or condensed directory for supplication have ever been sufficiently appreciated. It was the manner of Jesus to instruct by example; and by this type-form He certainly sought to impress upon the mind of His subjects in all subsequent ages that they should address themselves to prayer as a real, and, though reverential, yet most confiding, converse with God as their holy and gracious Father; that their words to Him should be few, well ordered, and childlike; that, while they might humbly represent their immediate and most pressing earthly wants, what it chiefly became them to beg at His hand was deliverance from His displeasure and from sin; but that, before all personal mercies, it was their priest-like privilege as God's children to enter with sympathy into His own large thoughts of love for all mankind, and to seek what He seeks, the manifestation of His glory by the reduction of the world into obedience to His perfect will. For no other exercise of worship, except the sacraments, did the Son of God think it worth while to prescribe a model. But He Who found in prayer the means of keeping up in His strange human exile and at the distance of our earth that most intimate and tender intercourse which He had with His eternal Father before love drew Him into flesh, stooped patiently to teach us how by prayer we too, 'who sometime were far off' and shut out from God, might reopen communications with the Unseen, and become active members of that spiritual family whose Head is glad to hearken when His children speak and prompt to answer when they ask. This Elder Brother never looked more touching in His lowliness than when He dictated in brief and easy words the prayers of us sinful men to our Father Who is in heaven. Such prayers are as far removed from the folly of superstition as from the falsehood of hypocrisy.

PART II.

EXCURSUS.

Eph. ii. 13.

# THIRD APPLICATION:

TO FASTING.

Moreover, when ye fast, be not, as the hypocrites, of a sad countenance: for they disfigure their faces that they may appear unto men to fast. Verily, I say unto you, They have their reward. But thou, when thou fastest, anoint thine head and wash thy face; that thou appear not unto men to fast, but unto thy Father Which is in secret: and thy Father Which seeth in secret shall reward thee openly.—MATT. VI. 16-18.

THIRD APPLICATION: TO FASTING.

ABSTINENCE for a time, either from all food or from a free indulgence in it, or from the more pleasant kinds of it, is an expression of grief so very natural as in some instances to become involuntary. The man whose whole life is taken possession of by a recent and severe calamity cannot eat as at other times, even if he would. No real mourner will be nice in his choice of viands, although he may consent to still the cravings of hunger. Abstinence, therefore, partial or total, becomes part of that natural language by which men have always striven to express in their behaviour the grief of their heart. It may be grief accompanied by indignation, like Jonathan's at the furious envy of his father against his friend David; or grief accompanied by anxiety, such as David's own when his infant's life hung in the balance; or the grief of prolonged disappointment, as when Hannah mourned her want of children; or the grief of vexation and alarm which consumed Darius during the sleep-

[Side notes: PART II. THIRD APPLICATION. 1 Sam. xx. 34. 2 Sam. xii. 16. 1 Sam. i. 7. Dan. vi. 18.]

PART II.
THIRD APPLICATION.

less night when his first officer of state lay in a den of lions: for abstinence is natural under any of those emotions which are at once overmastering and depressing. Or the fast may be adopted in that species of social mourning, as for a public disaster or a private bereavement, which seeks expression in ways more or less conventional. The troops of the ten tribes fasted after their defeat in the old civil war against Benjamin; the population of Jabesh fasted for a week after the fatal fight in which the king fell at Gilboa.

Judg. xx. 26.
1 Sam. xxxi. 13; cf. 2 Sam. i. 12, iii. 35.

From instances like these, one passes naturally to fasting as an accompaniment of religious exercises. Men accustomed to express other kinds of grief by abstinence from their wonted meals will naturally adopt the same expression for devout sorrow on account of sin. In this way fasting has passed into the religious usages of worshippers in many lands and under various faiths. For sanitary reasons, dependent chiefly on climate and customary diet, it has been most prevalent among orientals. Rare in ancient Greece, it was frequent among the Egyptians and Persians, as it is to this day throughout Mohammedan countries.[1] It could hardly fail to find a place in the religious rites of the Palestine

[1] Cf. Winer, *Realwörterbuch*, sub voce.

Hebrews, even if it had been entirely passed over in their divine statute-book. It was not entirely passed over; but it seems to suggest how prevailingly cheerful, almost idyllic, was the tone of national worship during the earliest age of Judaism, that, while Moses was directed to enjoin several feasts, he enjoined no more than one fast in the sacred year. The great day of annual expiation or atonement was the solitary occasion which called on the whole people to 'afflict (or humble) their souls,' as the law phrased it,[1] by public fasting; of any private or individual acts of abstinence, save in one incidental allusion, the law had not a word to say. With all its rudeness, the first age of Israel's national existence was a glad age;[2] the memory of the Exodus and of the Conquest was still a spring of healthy exultation to the pious and patriotic. And though, under the troublous times of the later monarchy, we find on some few occasions a special public fast proclaimed by the authorities, as before the great war in Jehoshaphat's reign; yet these

PART II.
THIRD APPLICATION.

Lev. xvi. 29-31, xxiii. 27-32; Num. xxix. 7; alluded to, Acts xxvii. 9.

Num. xxx. 13.

2 Chron. xx. 3.

---

[1] This expression, which is used in the texts cited on the margin in the sense of 'fasting,' serves to explain the fuller phraseology of later passages, such as Isa. lviii. 5, Ezra viii. 21 (cf. ix. 5), and Ps. xxxv. 13.

[2] Of its 'rudeness' the Book of Judges is evidence enough; of its idyllic gladness in spite of trouble, the Book of Ruth.

occasions even are rare,¹ and there is no evidence that any other recurring fast, annual or weekly, was added to the one ordained by Moses, until the long captivity had come to embitter at last the spirit of the nation and to break its heart. Then indeed fasts, both public and private, both occasional and stated, became only too common. The captives themselves, like Daniel at Babylon and Esther in Persia, the great leaders of the return, like Ezra and Nehemiah, were all of necessity mourners for the national sins which had brought down the visitation of Jehovah; and they all joined fasting with those confessions, tears, and prayers, by which they sought to entreat the returning favour of their country's alienated God. From one of the prophets of the restoration we learn that four new annual fast-days had been instituted to commemorate the sad events of the captivity; one of which it was proposed to abolish after the long desolate temple had been at length

Margin notes: PART II. THIRD APPLICATION. Dan. ix. 3, x. 3; Esther iv. 3, 16; Ezra viii. 21–23, ix. 5, x. 6; Neh. i. 4, ix. 1. Zech. viii. 19, c. vii. 1 ff.

---

¹ There is one instance as early as Samuel, on occasion of one of the numerous reforms from idolatry (1 Sam. vii. 6); but except two allusions of doubtful date in the prophets (for a famine, in Joel i. 14, ii. 15; and that in Isa. lviii. 3 ff.) no other genuine case occurs till the fifth year of Jehoiakim (Jer. xxxvi. 6–10), when the realm had already been made tributary to Babylon. For the fast under cover of which Queen Jezebel compassed the murder of Naboth cannot be reckoned as a genuine exercise of worship (see 1 Kings xxi. 9–12).

rebuilt. To these were probably added, not long after, the two weekly fasts, on the observance of which self-righteous Pharisees of our Lord's day laid stress: the fasts, that is to say, of the second and fifth days in each week, for which the Christian Church at an early date substituted the fourth and sixth days. Nor did even this frequency of stated fasts supersede either the occasional appointment of others by authority or the practice of private fasting on personal grounds. It should be observed, however, that the exercise did not always involve entire abstinence from food.[1] When it did so, the time of abstinence was not protracted beyond one day, reckoned from sunset to sunset, and was therefore at once followed by the accustomed evening meal. A strict abstinence of this duration, which really amounted in many cases to the omission only of a single meal, was not, in a warm climate and among a rather inactive people, at all injurious to health. Where the fast consisted only in a prolonged disuse of wine and flesh, the exercise was probably to be recommended for dietetic reasons.

PART II.
THIRD APPLICATION.
Luke xviii. 12.

See Grotius on Luke l. c.

Cf. Josephus, *Vita*, 56.

Cf. Dan. x. 3.

Joseph. *Antt.* iii. 10. 3.

Cf. Dan. i. 3–16.

---

[1] The Roman Catholic Church has adopted a similar division of fasts into (1) *jejunium*, which means entire abstinence from one evening to the next; and (2) *abstinentia*, which only means the absence of flesh-meat from the diet. See Herzog, *Encyklopädie*, sub voce.

PART II.
———
THIRD
APPLICATION.

When fasting assumes a religious character, such as we have thus seen to belong to it throughout Hebrew history, it may be said to aim at two distinct and separable results. Its first value is simply that of a natural expression for sorrow. It allies itself with the squalid visage, the unwashed person, the coarse sackcloth or rent robe, the dust thrown over the head, the beating of the breast, and other demonstrations of violent affliction usual among orientals.[1] Transferred to exercises of religious penitence, it is designed to give utterance to the deep depression of the heart on account of sin. Of course, its value as a symbol of religious mourning must depend, first, on the genuineness of the mourning to be expressed; and next, on the fitness of this particular symbol to express it. Religious life, like all human life, has its alternations of depression and of joy; and to be thoroughly natural, it must find for both becoming forms of expression. But the law of truth is obviously transgressed when in obedience to custom or prescription the forms of religious grief are observed by men whose real feelings at the moment are bright and cheerful

[1] See a good summary of these, as practised by the Hebrews and other allied races, in the Art. 'Mourning,' in Smith's *Dict. of the Bible.*

This is the principle of our Lord's reply to the question respecting fasts put to Him by the followers of John the Baptist. It could not fail to strike the contemporaries of Jesus that the religious temper of His disciples was precisely the reverse of that which characterized all the other eminent schools of piety embraced within the faith of Israel. The Pharisees, who inherited in exaggerated form the traditions of the age that succeeded the exile; the Essenes, whose rule was still stricter and more ascetic; and, the scholars of the great Baptizer, whose mission it had been to call his countrymen to a preparatory repentance: all these signalized their exceptional piety by exceptional austerities. Religion was with them a thing of gloom, of self-mortification, and of abstinence. In singular contrast stood Jesus and His scholars. They neither fasted nor shunned society, but mixed freely in social life and cultivated a cheerful affability of manner. The justification of this change Jesus found simply in its reason: they feasted because they were glad; to fast was impossible for them, because as yet they were not sad. To use John's own figure, they were chosen comrades of Him Who is the heavenly Bridegroom of all pure and loving hearts, and Whose coming made a bright

PART II.

THIRD APPLICATION.
Matt. ix. 14, 15; Mark ii. 18–20; Luke v. 33–35.

Cf. Matt. and Mark, *l.c.*

See John iii. 29.

P

wedding-day in the spiritual life of every one who received Him. You cannot make men fast for sorrow, when God is satisfying them with the new wine of His kingdom as with the joy of marriage.[1] But these first followers were not to stand always on the hill-top of joy. On fruition and the filling up of a long-deferred hope there were to follow loss and the pain of absence. The death of Jesus (thus early foreseen by Himself) came to make all their world dark again and emptier than before; and then, for at least the brief 'day' which found them 'orphans,' there were none in Israel so ready to fast as they, over Him Who had been snatched from their eyes. These things are a picture of all christian life: for, though the coming of the Second Comforter has given to the experience of Christians under the New Testament a more prevailing accent of cheerfulness than was ever possible before, and made it each believer's duty, in St. Paul's words, to 'rejoice evermore;' yet such joy must still depend on the presence of 'the Bridegroom' realized by faith, and may still be forfeited, when, through unbelief or disloyalty, the

Margin notes: PART II. THIRD APPLICATION. Cf. Luke, l.c. — John xiv. 18, Greek. — John xiv. 16. — 1 Thess. v. 16; cf. Phil. iv. 4.

---

[1] It was surely to symbolize this new feature in His kingdom that our Lord led His earliest converts to Cana, and there first 'manifested forth His glory.'—John ii. 1-11.

soul has to mourn a temporary withdrawal or eclipse of His gracious face. Dark hours in which remembered failure and unfaithfulness and the breach of holy purposes crowd in to obscure one's spirit, and if they do not alarm with fear of apostasy, at least succeed in shutting out everything but that 'hope' which clings like a 'sure and stedfast anchor' to the Forerunner, Whose very absence means that He has entered for us behind the veil; these are the hours when you cannot force christian men to be glad, but must suffer them to indulge in an inward fast.

<small>PART II. THIRD APPLICATION.</small>

<small>Heb. vi. 18–20.</small>

Whether in any case this inward fast of a mournful heart is to be reflected in outward abstinence from pleasant food will depend on health, personal habits, and local usage. A change of diet which is safe for people leading an outdoor life in a warm climate, may be very hurtful to the over-strained and seldom over-fed population of our cities. Again, it suits the emotional East to tear the robe and beat the breast for sorrow; it does not suit the self-restrained Englishman. So the bread of sorrow, eaten with tears, may be, like a sad-coloured dress, a natural enough accompaniment of penitence among a people who love to do everything in public and to mirror every mood of mind in fitting external symbol; it may be most unnatural to us. We have retained indeed the disuse of colour in our dress as an expression of mourning; but we apply it only to mourning for the dead; and in almost everything else we have abandoned the attempt to speak our emotions to the public eye by either badge or gesture or deportment. Even the language of facial expression in which nature teaches childhood to betray its feelings, we tutor ourselves to suppress or to disguise. While therefore it may be a natural, and, to some races, a seemly token of inward grief, the fast is certainly as much out of place among ourselves, and as foreign to our national tastes, as it would be to shave our heads or sit for a week in silence on the ground.

Cf. Job ii. 13.

To say this, however, is not to exhaust the religious significance of fasting. If it began to be numbered among the adjuncts of devotion for the sake of its expressiveness, it soon came to be employed for the sake of its effects. It is first a sign of grief: it is also a discipline of the soul. To impose at certain times a stricter limit upon the indulgence of appetite than temperance imposes at all times, with a view either to chasten those desires which have their seat in the body or to leave the spiritual nature more free for prolonged and absorbed worship, has always been recognised as legitimate, and employed as a wholesome discipline by those who have aspired to a life of purity and devotion. It has been practised with this design by worshippers under nearly every creed and in almost every age of the world. It is, in fact, the true and useful measure of self-denial, of which asceticism has been the wide-spread abuse.¹ Every man who desires to use his body as an instrument in the service of God will strive to respect under all circumstances those rules of moderation in the gratification of his appetites which are prescribed by health, by purity, by sobriety, and by the subordination of the animal in man to the control of reason and of conscience. Within these rules, however, there is permissible a certain latitude of ordinary indulgence in the lower pleasures of the body, which very well consorts with the cheerful and thankful

---

¹ Does not asceticism begin only at that point where the refusal of any bodily gratification or the self-infliction of bodily suffering is believed to possess a necessary spiritual value of its own, apart from properly spiritual conditions; whether that value be supposed to lie in meriting divine commendation or in effecting moral reformation? Popularly indeed the word is commonly applied also to cases in which an exaggerated value is ascribed to self-denial as a means to spiritual or moral results, even though no proper or inherent virtue is believed to belong to it.

spirit, habitual to the Christian. He Who came 'eating and drinking,' has taught His followers to hold every creature of God for good, 'if it be received with thanksgiving,' and to use, without abusing, our Father's gifts with a freedom which could not be safely granted to man till men had become sons of God. This freedom no Christian is at liberty to surrender to the judgment of any 'weaker brother' or at the bidding of any ecclesiastical authority. But there do come seasons in the inward life of the soul, known only to each devout person and to be judged of by himself alone, when the higher wants of the divine life will be best served by a voluntary abdication of this liberty and a self-imposed abstinence from permitted pleasures. It may be that some secret lust, fed by a full habit of body or taking advantage of the too easy humours bred by self-indulgence, needs to be weakened, mortified, and by a wholesome severity tamed into subjection; and the christian athlete may do wisely to forestall the sharper discipline of divine affliction by 'keeping under' his own body. Eminently this is a case in which, to use Bishop Jeremy Taylor's words, 'a man may abate of his ordinary liberty and bold freedom with great prudence, so he does it without singularity in himself, or trouble to others.' It may be, on the other hand, that instead of being in danger of falling below the normal purity of a Christian, the saint is summoned by God's dealings with him to a certain unwonted elevation of spiritual experience. All healthy religion is liable to its Peniels, like Jacob ; to its crises of spiritual struggle : and the highest lives have sometimes been called to go up, like Moses, to some Sinai-summit, or driven, like Elijah, unto Horeb, or even led in the footsteps of a Greater still into a wilderness of temptation. When the human spirit would brace itself for such extraordinary seasons of divine communion, would draw into itself the highest measure of divine strength for exceptional efforts, or would pass through inward victory to a serener and heavenlier life than it has been wont to lead ; all experience teaches that the intrusive calls and grosser motions of the flesh must be for the time denied, and to fast becomes the natural preparative and the concomitant of prayer. Our Lord's forty days' seclusion after baptism, prefigured in the history of Moses and Elijah, is at once the type-example and the supreme justification of all lesser instances.

The service which occasional abstinence by persons in full health may thus render as 'a

[Marginalia: PART II. THIRD APPLICATION. Gen. xxxii. 24–30. Ex. xxiv. 18; 1 Kings xix. 8; Matt. iv. 1, 2.]

Part II.

Third Application.
Jeremy Taylor, *ut supra*.

See p. 221, margin and footnote.

nourishment of prayer, a restraint of lust, and an instrument of humility,' probably lies at the bottom of that Pentateuch expression for fasting which reappears in later Hebrew—I mean the 'afflicting of the soul.' The soul is 'afflicted,' humbled¹ or brought down, when the body is made feeble by a low diet; and though this may refer only to the expression of religious grief, it seems more natural to see in such a phrase a recognition of the effects of abstinence, as a discipline, upon the spiritual life. No doubt such physical aid to self-culture and especially to self-humbling must always be used with much carefulness and under the most judicious safeguards. No doubt it may very easily become a minister to superstition, be pushed the length of asceticism, or generate the spiritual 'pride which apes humility.' At the same time, it can never be

Cf. Ps. lxix. 10.²

urged as a 'reproach' against any devout and humble worshipper that in his longing after purity and divine fellowship he adopts such a

---

¹ The Septuagint equivalent is ταπεινοῦν τὴν ψυχήν; whence '*humbled my soul*' in Ps. xxxv. 13.

² The three psalms in which reference is made to fasting (xxxv. 13, lxix. 10, and cix. 24) are all ascribed to David, with more or less probability. In Psalm lxix. the fasting is evidently part of the psalmist's humiliation for dishonour done to God. In Psalm cix. it is not clear that religious fasting is meant; but the physical feebleness produced by it is described.

subordinate assistance, except by the profane. Our Lord Himself gave His express sanction to this conjunction of fasting with prayer whenever the faith which works miracles is required to be exalted into extraordinary potency. 'This kind,' He said, by way of explaining why His apostles had failed in their effort to exorcise the demon from an epileptic and lunatic boy—'This kind goeth not out but by prayer and fasting.' Whatever else these remarkable words may carry, they certainly assume that abstinence from food during seasons of prayer is among the legitimate means by which in certain cases the religious faith of the soul may be brought into its highest and most powerful activity. It was thus the apostles were taught by the Spirit to understand their Master. Both by example and express permission, they gave fasting a place among the rarer exercises of christian life. When the primitive Church was called to acts of special solemnity and moment, such as the selection of missionaries or the ordination of presbyters, it engaged in an extraordinary service of worship, accompanied with fasting. Similar seasons of exceptional devotion, under abstinence from the gratification of the appetites, are recognised by St. Paul as equally permissible to the private believer.

Margin notes:
PART II. THIRD APPLICATION.
Matt. xvii. 21; cf. Mark ix. 29, where the reading wavers, however.
See Acts xiii. 3, xiv. 23.
1 Cor. vii. 5. But the *textus receptus* is here doubtful.

PART II.
THIRD
APPLICATION.

The evidence of the New Testament, however, and, on the whole, that of the Old also, is rather unfavourable to the imposition of stated, obligatory, and general fasts. The formal recurrence of fast-days in every week, the annual observance of Lent, and the custom of fasting before receiving the Lord's Supper (of which the first two at least grew up within the Church of the first three centuries, and even passed at the Reformation into Protestant worship), appear somewhat inconsistent both with the joyous tone of the christian economy and with the rare, casual, and optional character which properly belongs to this exercise. For I believe the impression which is made by the whole teaching of Scripture on this subject is that (apart from the oriental use of a spare diet as one of the natural signs of grief) religious fasting is mainly a personal discipline, to be employed at the discretion of the individual just in so far as he may find it to be a help to his devotions under exceptional circumstances, and especially at any unusually solemn crisis in his religious history. There certainly does not appear to be any sufficient reason for the recent decline and disuse of this ancient discipline among all classes, and, so far as I am aware, throughout the whole of the Protestant communions. Modern Christianity has become predominantly active, aggressive, and beneficent. Religious people now-a-days live upon the outgoings of their faith in works of charity. The cultivation of purely devotional piety has correspondingly declined; and fasting, as a discipline of devotion, has gone out of use, along with questions for self-examination, cases of casuistry, rules of life, and other aids or guides to a scrupulous and contemplative piety. The change is partly an improvement; but surely not wholly so. It is never a safe thing to over-cultivate one side of religion; and we are in danger of losing depth, reverence, tenderness, and humility, through our one-sided activity in doing, rather than in being, good. A better balance in the development of christian life would find room for self-discipline, penitential fasting, and protracted seasons of private communion with God, alongside of those practical engagements which are at present so multifarious and absorbing; and christian life would be all the stronger as well as more symmetrical for the combination.

What is abundantly clear from the very nature of a fast is that it is not a thing to be paraded before one's neighbours. It is entirely a subsidiary

PART II.

THIRD APPLICATION.

aid to spiritual exercises, of no value in itself. It finds its justification usually in something quite personal to the individual, with which no one else need have anything to do. It is too exceptional to form part of men's stated acts of worship; nor can its observance by one person be any rule for another. No doubt a hypocrite will find the temptation to make capital out of his fast-days a strong one, just because to keep fasts is supposed to be a mark of unusual seriousness and depth of piety. Still most men will feel that there is a peculiar indecency in thrusting private exercises of so personal and sacred a character on the notice of onlookers. This instance of Pharisaic ostentation outdoes those which have been already rebuked by Christ. It was really a new thing, even in Jewish hypocrisy. More than one of the old prophets had chastised the insincerity of public fasts for sin, which were not accompanied by any reform of manners or any 'fruits meet for repentance.' But there is no earlier trace in Hebrew literature of men who took care to call attention to the fact that they either were, or affected to be, keeping a private fast, by the studiously disfigured and neglected aspect of their persons. To make believe that one is deeply exercised about one's sins, and have an eye all the while

See Isa. lviii. 3–8; Zech. vii. 5–14; and perhaps Mal. iii. 14 (cf. ver. 5). Similar is Ecclus. xxxiv. 26.

to what people will say about such eminent godliness, betrays a singularly hardened or besotted religious nature.

But Jesus is hardly content, in this third instance, to apply His law of secrecy in worship, in precisely the same way as in the two previous instances. He does not say, merely, When thou fastest, enter into thy closet, and fast in secret before thy Father: but He bids us positively conceal all traces and signs of fasting before we return to the society of our fellows. 'Anoint thine head, and wash thy face,' must mean: Be careful to observe the ordinary rules of social life, and to assume before others your customary aspect of cheerfulness. The heart may be heavy enough through that bitterness of sin within it which is known to none else; and in the secret exercises through which we are forced to pass in our solitary hours, the body, sympathizing with the spirit, may refuse its pleasant food to eat the bread of tears: no matter; such painful self-scrutiny and mortification of secret lust is too much out of harmony with the buoyant attitude of normal and healthy christian life to be obtruded by any visible token upon the attention of our brethren. We are not called as a saved society to sorrow, but to gladness. Such inward

PART II.

THIRD APPLICATION.

Ps. lxxx. 5.

mourning as calls for a fast is characteristically an exceptional personal thing which comes of the evil in the individual heart. It has no business to throw its black shadow across the souls that have been redeemed for joy. It is due to the comfort of Christians whose inner life is better than our own, due to the courtesies dictated by unselfish regard for others, and due to the Lord of Gladness Himself, that he who for his sins must fast in secret should at least come forth with every trace of tears washed off, and no ill-favoured downcast look to mar the cheerfulness of the outside world. Few people now-a-days are given to a literal fasting; yet so long as religious life must have its side of austerity and gloom, so long will there be good people who sin against this law. Some Christians have always been found to betray their prevailing seriousness by sour visages, whining tones, or meekly melancholy eyes. Unless such trappings of an unattractive piety are falsely assumed, we dare not say that Christians of this class are the modern representatives of the sad-countenanced men whom our Lord condemned. But we may say, that they have not laid to heart the principle of His law which requires that penitential grief should be kept to oneself and to God. So far from affecting a misery you do not feel, or parading in society the religious melancholy which you think sits well on the devout, you ought to conceal such grief when it has become inevitable, lest it make discord with that note of joy to which all godly life has now been more than ever set. That is a reasonable violence, which a good man does to his private feelings when he restrains the utterance of religious depression, lest he should oppress without cause some heart which God hath not made sad, or check the smile which God has put on childhood's lips, or asperse the joy of Christ's redeemed by making earth a cloudier, sadder place than it needs to be. God knows, it is sad enough and cloudy enough at the best; let the Christian keep his sorrow, with his fasting, to himself, but hold it for a christian duty to shed abroad wherever he goes the 'great joy' which of right belongs to the 'glad tidings' of our salvation. Luke ii. 10.

PART II.
THIRD APPLICATION.

THE END.

www.ingramcontent.com/pod-product-compliance
Lightning Source LLC
Chambersburg PA
CBHW020807230426
43666CB00007B/892